HAUNTED CEMETERIES
OF
NEW ENGLAND

Stories, Stones, & Superstitions

Roxie J. Zwicker

PublishingWorks, Inc.
Exeter, NH
2009

"Song for Margaret," by Dan Lindner, from I'll Take the Hills—Banjo Dan's Songs of Vermont. It may be ordered through the Banjo Dan website, www.banjodan.com

PublishingWorks, Inc.
151 Epping Road
Exeter, NH 03833
603-778-9883

For Sales and Orders:
1-800-738-6603 or 603-772-7200

Designed by: Anna Pearlman

LCCN: 2008926952
ISBN: 1-933002-82-4
ISBN-13: 978-1-933002-82-8

Printed on recycled paper.

To my husband, Ken, may our paths travel side by side forever.

We miss you, Phil. May you find the peace you seek.

TABLE OF CONTENTS

INTRODUCTION

It was during my friend's birthday party that I realized it. I was maybe ten or eleven, and amidst the colorful presents and tempting boxes of vibrant crayons, I saw it there. In Williamsburg, Massachusetts, next to my friend Sara's house, there was a large cemetery. The excitement of going in for a visit was so tempting. I wasn't sure why, but there seemed to be a fascination that needed to be acknowledged. Finally, when the drinks and the cake were finished and the gifts were piled high with crumpled wrapping paper at our feet, we were ready. We climbed through the low bushes (there was no gate; bushes were the only barrier between the burial ground and her house) that bordered the yard, and at the edge of the cemetery we just stood and stared. I remember taking the first steps on to the well-manicured lawn, looking around, and then making our way around the gravestones.

It wasn't a terribly old cemetery, maybe a hundred years old or so at the time. We curiously looked around at the mementos placed on some of the stones and the flowers that had been left behind and we wondered how long it had been since someone had visited these graves. How long had it been since someone stood there and remembered, since they cried, since they were thought of? I recall finding one large marble stone for a child who had passed away around the age of five. For some reason, the thought came to me to lean over the stone and embrace it, almost as if I was embracing the child. As I felt the cold stone against me, I could feel a tingling through my upper body radiating from the stone. I closed my eyes to be sure of what I was feeling, to be completely in the moment. When I opened my eyes, I still felt the same sensation. Sara came over and looked at me rather puzzled. I asked her to put her hands on the stone, too. Almost as quickly as she touched the stone, she pulled her hands back, and I knew she had felt it, too. She then turned and started to run back to her house. I hesitated for just a moment, and then I followed after Sara. We crossed back through the bushes, then she stopped and turned to look at me, then all she said was, "I felt it, too."

I believe I can mark the eerie experience I had in that western Massachusetts graveyard as the beginning of my fascination with cemeteries. I have managed to travel New England from corner to corner seeking out old burial places, and if I were to count, I think the number of cemeteries I've explored numbers somewhere over two hundred. During my adventures I've learned many things from these captivating places. Gravestones have shared their epitaphs with me like forgotten poems that reside in dusty books on library shelves. The artwork and hand-carved details have shown me a world of folk art covering everything from representations of the devil to interpretations of the gates of heaven. The spirits that occupy these places, whether friendly or alarming, just want you to know that they are there—even when you don't want them to.

The word "remember" means so much more when you've spent time in these gardens of stone. As a visitor to a graveyard, you are part of the progression of time. Someone has traveled these somber lanes before you and left someone they cared for behind. Will you stop and remember them? Even though you may be a complete stranger to the souls that are buried in these places, you came by to consider the existence of the departed. If you've ever stopped to read the worn epitaphs or touch the engravings, your thoughts connect with what's in front of you, and who is buried below.

Is it strange to think that these places have a spiritual energy to them where the souls would want to make themselves known? Imagine the comfort in knowing that those who we've loved and lost are in a spirit world where they look back at us and remember. These graves represent people like you and I who possessed emotion, curiosity, and memory. If you had the opportunity to come back and reconnect, would you? We each have countless reasons why we might like to come back and check in with those still living. Think of the emotions that might be tied to these reasons, including the desire to find the ones we've loved. Often, the emotional need to connect with people who have affected our lives remains in our memories, whether happy or sad. Would it be a stretch to think that our memories would not follow us in the afterlife?

There are many people I've met who have told me that my cemetery curiosity is a bit morbid. While it is true that I've come across some peculiar things in my travels, I've never considered my interest morbid. Each place, no matter how large or small, holds a fascination, as there is always something to offer. Walking through cemeteries can introduce visitors to the history of a town or city, and much can be discovered by reading the gravestone inscriptions of a community's former inhabitants. I've been so moved in some burial grounds that I would sometimes sit down in front of the stones and remain there peacefully, lost in thought. Other times, I've run back to my car to find something to leave on the grave, a token to say that I was here—and I remembered you.

I have done numerous lectures on New England cemeteries, and often afterwards I'll have crowds of people talking to me at length about their own graveyard adventures, or about an unusual stone they've found. They've made the connection with the past, activated by something, somewhere. I always encourage them to continue exploring, and I'll often give advice on places to go check out locally. Curiosity is one of the best qualities you can have while visiting old graveyards.

Of course, living in New England there is no escape from old cemeteries. From the family plots in isolated farm fields to crowded burial grounds in the state capitals, gravestones mark the earlier days of our history—and what a history it is! Where else can you go and physically touch a relic of the past that might be two-hundred or three-hundred years old? Certainly New England boasts some of the finest museums in the nation, with artifacts that date much earlier than the settlement of America. However, New England's graveyards are places to connect with the tales and, in many cases, the ghosts of those who came before us.

Some of the earliest ghost stories we are told as children are in cemetery settings. Nothing seems more frightening than the dark of the night in an old burial ground. The uneven qualities of the grounds, with old gnarled tree roots twisting up through the soil and with the dramatic carvings of cherubs and skulls on the headstones, make graveyards even more dramatic. That prickly feeling can easily be aroused as the darkness builds in the necropolis of the dead, and sometimes you can't help but have all of your senses heightened just a degree or two.

Bring your sense of adventure and an open mind as we venture through some of the oldest burial grounds in New England and visit with their resident specters. We will venture past the rusty iron gates and through the swaying tall grasses as we get up close with the ghosts and graveyards that are just waiting to share their secrets with you.

CONNECTICUT

UNION CEMETERY, EASTON

Like stars that struggle through the clouds of night,
Thine eyes one moment caught a glorious light,
As if to thee, in that dread hour, 'twere given
To know on earth what faith believes of heaven ;
Then like tired breezes didst thou sink to rest,
Nor one, one pang the awful change confess'd.
Death stole in softness o'er that lovely face,
And touch 'd each feature with a new-born grace ;
On cheek and brow unearthly beauty lay,
And told that life's poor cares had pass'd away.
—Charles Sprague, "Lines On The Death Of M.S.C."

O ne of the most infamous burial grounds in the state of Connecticut is the Union cemetery, located in the town of Easton, easily located at the junction of Route 136 and Route 59. This is the domain of the ghost known as the "White Lady." Stories have been told about this specter for long over fifty years, and the interest in her story is probably more popular today than ever. Paranormal groups find themselves drawn to the story and to the graveyard to try and catch a glimpse of this active spirit. There is so much fascination with the haunted tale that the local police have to regularly patrol the graveyard and escort would-be ghost chasers out.

The White Lady is said to not only inhabit the Union cemetery, but she has been rumored to travel the road to nearby Stepney graveyard in Monroe, Connecticut. The identity of the White Lady is unknown, but there are many theories as to who she might be. One of the legends is that the spirit could be that of

Ellen Smathers, wife of John Smathers, whose body was discovered near the graveyard, buried in a sinkhole behind the adjacent Easton Baptist Church. When his body was recovered, it was weighted down with heavy iron pieces. A man named Richard Dean Jason confessed to the murder and was sentenced to life in prison. The theory was that Jason murdered John Smathers in hopes of having a romantic relationship with Ellen. During his remaining days in prison, Jason told other prisoners about a mysterious shadow man that he encountered around the time of the murder, which only leaves more questions about the story. There is also another theory that the white lady could be Mrs. Knott, whose body was discovered in this same sinkhole behind the church, murdered and dumped there by her adulterous lover, Elwood Wade. Both of the murder victims are buried in the Easton cemetery.

The burial ground is said to be an attraction for a variety of spirits besides the White Lady, perhaps drawn to the energies that are there, making it an active spot for these specters. Stories have been told that many cemetery visitors have reported actually having conversations with what seem to be people. These ghosts are said to look, talk, and act like living human beings, except for the fact that they vanish into thin air. There are numerous photographs of light anomalies, beams of solid light and eerie mists that have been taken by paranormal enthusiasts, who claim that these anomalies were not visible to the naked eye when taken.

Personal accounts of encounters with phantoms from the Easton cemetery are all too common. In a story told from 1993, Glenn Pennell, a local fireman, claims that the White Lady was walking in the middle of the road near the burial ground. The specter turned to look at Glenn and reached out her arms towards him. Shocked by what he had seen, he said that he accidentally hit her with his pickup truck. Even more peculiar was that the road turned into a cobblestone street before his eyes, and he seemed to drive right through the ghost. He even alleged that he heard a thump, and a dent on his truck became evidence of the encounter with the spirit. The spirit was described as wearing a white ruffled nightgown or dress with a bonnet and a single braid of hair. As if seeing the ghost of a woman in front of him wasn't enough, Glenn claimed to look in the passenger seat of his truck and saw a man sitting there wearing a straw hat.

There was a bit of speculation in regards to the firefighter's encounter with the ghosts on that dark night, and there were many people who claimed that it must have been his eyes playing tricks on him. To those who are familiar with the story, it was just further confirmation of her existence.

Lorraine and Ed Warren, founders of the New England Society for Psychic Research in 1952, were paranormal investigators that spent a considerable amount of time at the burial ground. The encounters that Lorraine and Ed documented at the cemetery seemed like some of the strongest evidence of spiritual activity to even the most skeptical. After a researcher for the society recorded the number 23 being repeated over and over in the cemetery when there was no one around one night, Ed Warren decided to investigate for himself.

Ed spent nearly a week at the Union Cemetery with a video recorder hoping to capture a glimpse of the White Lady. During that time he was able to record ghostly whispers in the cemetery and even photographed strange light anomalies. Ed was really hoping to capture something dramatic, a definitive piece of evidence that could not be disputed. Perseverance paid off on the seventh night around 2:00 a.m. when a strange glow started to take shape. The video taken that night revealed an amazing scene—the ghostly glow of lights came together to form the shape of a woman. She was described as having dark hair and she wore a flowing white gown. Stranger still, the white lady wasn't alone, she was surrounded by other dark spirits. Weird shapes of other beings swirled around her. The incessant sound of voices grew and it seemed as though these dark spirits were arguing with the lady. Yet the White Lady continued to walk towards Ed, despite the commotion. Ed stepped towards the lady, out in front of the camera, and as he approached her, she vanished. Did Ed capture the spirit of the White Lady on tape? Those who have viewed the tape seem to think so.

The Union Cemetery is quite simple in design, wide open and spacious, with the headstones all aligned in very neat rows. Some of the older stones date back to the 1700s and there is an assortment of the various funerary symbols of the time. There is a beautiful marble stone marker for Alanson Beers, who died at the age of twenty-two in 1870, that depicts a triangle with a star surrounded by Greek columns. Another beautiful marble marker with a gothic arch and vining leaves reads, "Hattie – We loved thee." There are many graves throughout the burial ground that simply have small stones and pebbles resting on the top of the headstones. While there are a handful of broken stones, most of the markers are still in very good shape, and the burial ground is still used today. A rusty iron fence surrounds the cemetery, and there is a posted sign reminding visitors that the burial ground is closed from sunset to sunrise, which happens to be the best time for ghost enthusiasts alike to catch a glance of one of Fairfield County's most famous ghosts.

PIKE'S HILL BURIAL GROUND, WOLCOTT

The hearts escape leads out to everywhere,
Nowhere, but dreams still find a certain black Connecticut Hill.
My grandfather stands tall
And wraps me in his cemetery cloak,
Encircles me against the nightmare chill,
Till gowned in fear I follow with his ghost
Through village, town, down through the midnight past.

—Ruth Whitman, "Touro Synagogue"

Located in New Haven County is the town of Wolcott, originally known as Farmingbury, a mostly residential small town. The first cemetery in town was established on Pike's Hill, a beautiful spot whose summit affords a magnificent view of the area. It was first established in 1774, but saw little use in the following years, when some of its graves were relocated to newly built cemeteries nearby.

The oldest known tombstone from this cemetery is Rachel Brockett's, who died at the young age of twenty-two on October 17, 1776. Her stone has a death's head skeleton carved at the top, and twisting scrollwork with leafy borders along the sides. The inscription on the stone reads:

> In memory of Rachel Brockett
> Who died Oct. ye 17th, 1776
> In ye 22nd year of her age.
> While you are blooming, young and spry,
> Perhaps you think you ne'er will die;

But here's a witness of the truth,
That you may die while in your youth.

A ghostly legend from the early eighteenth century exists about this burial ground. There had once been a house on top of Pike's Hill where an old, gruff man lived by the name of Horton. As the days of his old life waned, he spoke of not wanting to be buried in the old cemetery on Pike's Hill. "If you bury me in that lonely place, I will haunt you," Horton reportedly told local townsfolk. His request was ignored, however, and after his burial in the cemetery, visitors spoke of seeing his apparition walking among the graves. Over the years, more and more people saw the old man's unhappy spirit wandering about, as if he were searching for a way out of the cemetery. And since there was no fence around it, the notion of his spirit leaving to haunt the residents of the town increased the fears of the citizens of Farmingbury. The cemetery became known locally as the "haunted graveyard," and was avoided.

According to the book, *The Town and City of Waterbury, Connecticut*, by Joseph Anderson, published in 1896, there were only six stones in the graveyard that remained, the most recent was dated 1791. As the years progressed, the graveyard became overgrown, neglected, and completely forgotten.

A later book called *Connecticut: A Guide to Its Roads, Lore, and People*, published in 1938, mentions Pike's Hill cemetery briefly as a cut-through for hunters passing through the woods. At the time of that writing, the few remaining gravestones were barely visible beneath the tangle of brush and overgrowth of the woods. But now the peacefulness of the forest is all that can be found on Pike's Hill today, and memories of a long-forgotten burial ground that at one time was the most haunted place in town.

BARA-HACK VILLAGE
CEMETERY, CONNECTICUT

Now there is nothing but the ghosts of things, —
No life, no love, no children, and no men;
And over the forgotten place there clings
The strange and unrememberable light
That is in dreams. The music failed, and then
God frowned, and shut the village from His sight.

—*Edwin Arlington Robinson, "The Dead Village"*

Just an hour's drive from Hartford in the northeast corner of Connecticut is the small settlement of Pomfret in Windham County. In 1686, the land was obtained from the Indians for thirty pounds in what was known as the Mashamoquet Purchase. The Indian name "Mashamoquet" represented the largest stream that runs through Pomfret, and was designated as a great fishing place. Finally established in 1713, Pomfret was originally settled as a farming community. It has gained notoriety for the wolf's den, where the last wolf in Connecticut was killed by General Israel Putnam. Today the location has been placed on the national Register of Historic Places and is maintained as a state park. There is even a popular fishing spot in the area known as the Witches Woods Lake.

Lost in the woods near the large stream in Pomfret is the mysterious and forgotten village of Bara-Hack, a settlement that was founded by Dutch pioneer traders in 1790. The name "Bara-Hack" is said to have Dutch origins and means, "the breaking of bread." All that is left of the village today are gaping stone cellar holes and scattered, broken stone walls seemingly leading to nowhere. Underfoot are old stone wells and scattered rocks. The entire setting looks as though it came out of the backdrop of the movie *The Blair Witch Project*. Spooky, misshapen trees seem to reach out with their long, branched arms. There is also a strange carving on one of the rocks in the little village. It is of a face, but there seems to be no certainty as to when it was carved into the rock, or whom it depicts. There are many theories as to why the carving may exist: some people think that it is a marker for a sacred site. This stone face may go back to the time of the Native Americans and may hold great spiritual meaning and symbolism.

What happened to the inhabitants? Cemetery records reveal that the last burial took place around 1890. The stone markers here stand as memorials to three generations of the Higginbotham family who called this land home, and as a reminder of the quiet little village. In her book, *Folklore & Firesides in Pomfret, Hampton, and Vicinity*, Susan J. Griggs briefly recalls this family-based community:

> We read of the deserted villages of the cut-over lands of the northwest, but few know that Pomfret has its lost village where long ago the large family of Higginbothams lived and carried on a thriving business, their little mill being known as the Higginbotham Linen Wheels for hand spinning. The Higginbothams lived in their little settlement in the hills cultivating their fertile farms. Before the march of progress carried away the business of the little mill, their business prospered for three generations, and the thrifty inhabitants settled down by their comfortable firesides to enjoy the fruits of their life's labor, until they were, one by one, laid to rest in the little burying ground that they themselves had made ready and walled in against all intrusion; and there from the leaning headstones of their graves we learn the identity of these sturdy people.

Legend has it that Obadiah Higginbotham was stationed in Boston harbor during the Revolutionary War until March 17, 1776. He was thought to be a deserter from the British Army who escaped to Cranston, Rhode Island. Apparently, on October 5, 1778, Obadiah purchased ten acres of land from John Trowbridge in Pomfret for one hundred pounds. Then ten years later he bought adjacent land from Jonathan Randall for 120 pounds. On June 29, 1792, Obidiah joined the Woodstock Baptist church, and due to his different religious sentiments, he was dismissed from the Abington Congregational church on January 6, 1794. Today, a flax wheel made by Obadiah Higginbotham is part of the historic artifacts collection in Old Sturbridge Village, Massachusetts.

The village was abandoned some time after the Civil War. Some believe that the roads leading to town were just too long and the people decided to leave and move closer to the community. But there are others who believe that unusual activity may have frightened them away. There has been speculation that there were sightings of spirits during the times of the original settlement. One legend tells of spirits seen around the graveyard after the first interments occurred during the early nineteenth century. All that remains today in the cemetery are the gravestones and cellar holes.

The cemetery contains nine visible graves with the oldest grave for Phoebe, who was born November 8, 1783, and died November 21, 1802. It is possible that there are many more settlers that are buried in the cemetery, and their markers may have been lost to time. Several of the graves are quite tall and some have carvings of willow trees and urns on them. One grave belongs to Darius Higginbotham, who died on September 8, 1855, and also lists his two wives, Mary, who died at the age of twenty-eight, and Sally, who died at the age of seventy-five. The many inches of fallen leaves in the cemetery make rustling sounds while walking around the burial ground, however, if you stop to listen silently, you may hear sounds other than just leaves.

Bara-Hack is also known as the "village of voices" for the variety of ghostly sounds that have been heard over the years in the woods, sounds that cannot be traced to anything visual. It's been said that if you close your eyes while listening in the cemetery, you will be audibly transported back to the time when the village was inhabited. Children laughing and playing, cows mooing, dogs barking, and even a carriage traveling through the woods have all been heard on the grounds over the years. A book called *The Harvest of a Quiet Eye* written by Odell Shepard in 1927 tells the following about the village:

Here is the Village of Voices. For the place is peopled still … Although there is no human habitation for a long distance round about and no one goes there except the few who go to listen, yet there is always a hum and stir of human life … They hear the laughter of children at play … the voices of mothers who have long been dust calling their children into homes that are now mere holes in the earth. They hear vague snatches of song … and [the] rumble of the heavy wagons along an obliterated road. It is as though sounds were able in this place to get round that incomprehensible corner, to pierce that mysterious soundproof wall that we call Time.

Is stepping in Bara-Hack like journeying through a portal in time? Many people who have visited the village seem to think so. In the 1970s a group of college students conducted an investigation under the direction of Paul Eno, local folklorist and author. During this investigation the students became convinced that there was something otherworldly going on in the cemetery and in the village. Their account includes seeing full-bodied apparitions and hearing multiple voices while at Bara-Hack. Some of the group became lost in the burial ground during other investigations, although they had been there before. One member of the team became completely frozen in place on the trail into the woods and could not be physically moved by anyone there towards the direction of the cemetery.

A twisted Elm, just outside the graveyard wall, has its own tale; its roots have been burrowing into the ground underneath the cemetery for generations. The craggy branches have been seen cradling a baby, looking toward the burial ground. There is also the story of an old bearded man being sighted at the cemetery's west wall.

Logging is currently taking place in the woods around the village, and it is on private property, but even still it has generated quite a bit of interest for those who have had heard about this fascinating place. So, if you're planning a visit there, keep in mind the grounds are closely monitored for trespassers, by both the living and the dead.

OLD POQUETANOCK CEMETERY, PRESTON

O what an awful mystery!
O what a deep, deep history,
Hidden within us lies!
The spirit hath its unseen world,
And round it other spheres are whirl'd,
In its own mystic skies.
What restless aspirations—
What sense of limitations,
Live in it side by side!

—Henry Harbaugh, *"The Soul's Aspirations"*

Poquetanock is a sleepy little historic village in Preston, Connecticut, just outside the reach of the glittering lights of the Foxwoods casino. Once you've driven past the twinkling towers of the casino and the acres of parking lots, you will find the little township along Route 2A. In 1687, a tract of land lying between Norwich and North Stonington was deeded to Captain James Fitch, Captain Joshua Standish, and a number of other residents of the community from Oanaco, Sachem of the Mohegans. The town was called "New Preston" in the deed, named after an English town from which some families came; the name was eventually just shortened to Preston. The town of Preston consisted of just three populated areas and scattered farms. Each area—Preston City, Poquetanock, and Long Society—were typical, small New England villages, with services such as a blacksmith shop, a grist mill, and a store. Early trades practiced were tanning of leather and shoe making, including a silversmith, a goldsmith, and a clock maker. Even a number of small industries existed in Poquetanock, such as shipbuilding.

Bordering the road, numerous eighteenth-century homes welcome visitors, and each one exudes a charm that is so inviting, you would be tempted to stop in and visit the owners. Located atop a hill on Route 2A is the Captain Grant's Inn, a cozy retreat that seems lost in time. The Inn was originally built as a private home by Captain William Gonzales Grant in 1754 for his wife, Mercy Adelaide Avery. The Captain met his fate on the roaring seas of the Atlantic and his wife remained in the home for the rest of her days. Three generations of the Grant family continued to occupy the residence over the next 150 years. In fact, the house has a fascinating history as it was used as a soldier's garrison during the Revolutionary War, and during the Civil War, the home was used as part of the Underground Railroad assisting slaves. Today, the Inn is a charming bed and breakfast boasting wonderful, spirited tales of the ghosts who have taken up residence.

Behind the Inn is a spacious field used for farming in seasonable weather, and bordering the edges of the field are vast woods. At first glance there appears to be nothing but trees and thick brambles, but on a ridge high above a small rushing stream, the spirits of a forgotten cemetery are waiting to be discovered.

This abandoned graveyard quietly hides behind a fieldstone wall and presents a variety of challenges for visitors. If you can get past the fallen tree limbs and twisted thorny brambles, you can find a place that has succumed to the natural elements over time. The trees echo the presence of spirits in attendance. Branches on one tree sway although the air is still. In fact, a bizarre push and pull seems to affect most of the stones here. Fallen branches lean on the grave markers, while vines from the ground entwine themselves around the stones, pulling them into the ground. During the day it is a chilling place to visit. The pull of the vines at your clothing is like the touch of a bony corpse reaching from the grave, and the bending tree limbs overhead seem to move with every step that is taken in the cemetery. With the cover of bent and curling branches, there are infinite places for ghosts to hide.

Ted and Carol Matsumoto, owners of the Captain Grant's Inn, will sometimes bring curious guests out into the graveyard. What's fascinating about their occasional visits is that the paths between the graves change, almost from week to week. According to her, the cemetery is going through periods of self-cleansing. She explained to me that she notices new paths through the burial ground that were not visible on previous visits, as they were covered in thick vines, but she knew no one had been out there to clear them. Other times she described the grounds as completely impassable, with what seemed to be years of thick undergrowth that had appeared in just a short amount of time.

These confusing trails impede the curious who come to view the carvings and epitaphs in this lost place. There are over one hundred stones throughout the grounds, which have been abandoned for over forty years. The oldest deaths listed here date back to 1718, and the most recent stone dates from 1920. The carvings feature a number of Medusa head-style carvings with twirling hair that fans out in an electrified halo. However, there is so much decay on the headstones that many of them are barely legible anymore. Still the epitaphs that can be read here are poignant:

In memory of Mrs. Jennett Whipple, Wife of Joseph Whipple,
Who departed this life Oct 17, 1840, aged 85 years
How suddenly death's arrows fly
They strike us and pass not by
But hurt us to the grave
Learn wisdom from this solemn truth
That old must die and so may youth
No human power can save

A broken lamb rests on top of a tombstone that reads:

Gallup, John Mason, son of Henry J & Elizabeth Gallup
Here rests the body of our dear little boy
who fell asleep Aug 31, 1865,
Aged 4 years & 3 mo.
I'm going home

At night the burial ground has a surreal quality with the stones giving off a glow of strange shapes under the light of flashlights. Photographs taken in the graveyard at this time reveal orbs that are so well defined that shapes within the orbs can be seen. The theory behind orbs is that they represent the soul of a departed person, the essence of who they were in life, complete with intelligence, emotions, and personality.

The personality of this forgotten burial ground is ominous by day or night. Nature seems to be the only living force that is impacting this place, and from all appearances, quite often it seems like there hasn't been a soul who has visited here for years. Should you dare to visit, you will find a graveyard that is consumed by time, the environment, and phantoms of long ago.

MASSACHUSETTS

COPP'S HILL BURIAL GROUND, BOSTON

Show me your cemeteries and I'll tell you what kind of people you have.

—Ben Franklin

Copp's Hill Burying Ground is the second oldest burying ground in Boston, after King's Chapel. This is the largest graveyard in Boston and is located near the famous Old North Church. The grounds were named after William Copp, a former owner of the land, and many of his descendants are buried here. The British had once occupied Copp's Hill because of its strategic height and view, using it to train their cannons on Charlestown during the Battle of Bunker Hill. Now the hill is not as high as it used to be, being continually altered by man over the years.

The cemetery is comprised of four different sections: the Old North Burying Ground, Hull Street Burying Ground, Charter Street Burying Ground, and the New North Burying Ground. Each section was purchased at a separate time as the cemetery continued to expand over the years. It was estimated in 1882 that over ten thousand persons have been buried here. In the nineteenth century there were two hundred and thirty tombs, two belonging to the city of Boston. The tomb near Charter Street was said to have been fitted and prepared for children in June 1833. There are also purported to be thousands of free African Americans who lived in an area of Boston called New Guinea who are buried here as well, most of them in unmarked graves.

There are numerous stories of the desecration of graves in this cemetery. There are a handful of stones from the mid seventeenth century that had their dates altered by vandals who carved over the numbers, making the identification of the oldest stone in the burial ground difficult. The most common change was the modifying of 9s into 2s, so that a stone that read 1690 was changed to 1620. This happened in several of Boston's burial grounds.

Even more horrifying were tales of the displacement to the graves themselves. A woman who was a regular visitor to the graveyard said she saw heaps of coffins, stacked up, with visible remnants of their former occupants. Skin residue and even long black hair adhered to the caskets. It is alleged that these deeds were done by enterprising gravediggers seeking to maximize their profits from reusing the plots on the hill. No one was certain where the bodies were taken, but it was speculated that they were carted out of the cemetery in the middle of the night and dumped, one on top of another, and crushed into hideous masses to make additional room for more burials.

Tales of disinterment by those who were respected in the community were also fairly commonplace as well. One such story concerns Samuel Winslow, who was the church sexton in charge of the maintenance of the graveyard. The beautiful coat of arms on one tomb must have been appealing to Samuel, who had the bodies removed so he could use it as a temporary resting place for future burials. Samuel was so bold that he removed the name of William Clark from the tomb and had his own inscribed on there.

Another altered tomb was that of the Hutchinson family, situated near the southeast corner of the cemetery. A square slab of sandstone covers its entrance, and upon it is a beautiful coat of arms proudly displayed. The name of Hutchinson has been cutout and replaced with the name Thomas Lewis, who had no ties to the family. In the vault beneath this tablet once rested all that was mortal of Thomas Hutchinson, father of the Governor of Massachusetts during the time of the Stamp Act, and of Elisha Hutchinson, grandfather of His Excellency, the latter having fallen in an attack by Native Americans. They were descendants of Ann Hutchinson and her husband, Governor William. No one knows for sure where the final resting places of the Hutchinsons are today.

While there is a large assortment of gravestones from the seventeenth and eighteenth century, there have been many that have been carelessly lost for a variety of reasons. For example, in December of 1878, the superintendent of Copp's Hill opened an old tomb and discovered a headstone from 1713. The tomb had not been opened for eighteen years, and the undertaker who last closed it took standing gravestones to block the entrance before filling it in with dirt. Many stones will never see the light of day because they were placed in the bottoms of vaults for coffins to rest on.

In 1878, twenty-two grave markers that belonged to Copp's Hill were finally recovered. Two were being used as chimney tops, two covered drains, and others were found in the cellars of homes in the area. A tombstone was discovered when Commercial Street was being widened at the foot of Lime Alley, four feet below the surface. It's inscription read, "Elizabeth Boone, aged 2 years, Dyed ye 13 October 1677." These stones were randomly placed back in the burial ground, as there was no way to figure out where they truly belonged.

The terrain of the cemetery also presented challenges over the years. Dirt paths had to be concreted over as the rain washed away the soil creating gullies where the water collected. During heavy rains, so much dirt was washed away that the tops of coffins became visible.

During the nineteenth century, the cemetery was surrounded by tenement houses, and the tenants would string their clotheslines across the burial ground and attach them to the trees that stand inside the cemetery. The graveyard became overrun with house cats during those years.

There are various interesting stories about the inhabitants of the cemetery. One concerns a captain who was killed in Maine during an Indian assault. His body was riddled with bullets, which were removed and melted down. The lead was then poured into an opening on his slate grave marker. Over the years the metal has been hewn out with knives by neighborhood kids, leaving the slit filled with gravel and scant traces of lead. The stone can be found in the northwest section of the burial ground and the inscription reads:

CAPT THOMAS LAKE
AGED 61 YEERES
AN EMINENTLY FAITHFULL SERVANT
OF GOD & ONE OF A PUBLIC SPIRIT
WAS PERFIDIOUSLY SLAIN BY
ye INDIANS AT KENNIBECK
AUGUST ye 14th 1676
& HERE INTERRED THE 13 OF
MARCH FOLLOWING

A story about the "Wishing Rock" comes from the outer edges of the burial ground near the corner of Charter Street. The children used the flat surface of the rock as a playground, and they would dance in groups and sing around it as a means of sending forth their wishes. One day while the children were singing and circling the rock, the ground underneath them suddenly gave way and several of them fell into a forgotten underground well that opened up. The children were finally rescued by passersby.

Some notable people buried at Copp's Hill include Robert Newman, the Old North Church sextant who hung the lanterns on the night of Paul Revere's famous midnight ride. Another is Prince Hall, who is considered the founder of "Black Freemasonry." Fire and Brimstone preachers, Cotton and Increase Mather, are also buried in the ancient graveyard. Cotton Mather was a respected Boston minister who wrote on many religious topics. His 1689 book, *Memorable Providences*, describes a case of supposed witchcraft that had occurred in Boston the previous year. Three children had begun acting strangely after a disagreement with an Irish washerwoman, Mary Glover. After examining the children, Mather concluded that they were innocent victims of Glover's witchcraft. His sermons and written works fanned the flames of the witchcraft hysteria in Salem, Massachusetts. He declared that the Devil was at work in Salem, and that witches should face the harshest punishment.

The epitaphs here epitomize the sentiments of the times:

Sacred to the Memory of
MRS BETSEY PITMAN
wife to Mr Joseph Pitman
who departed this life March 8th, 1784
aged 27 years
Haste ! haste ! he lies in wait. He watches at the door.
Insidious Death ! Should his strong hand arrest,
No composition sets the prisoner free.
Death's terror is the mountain faith removes.
Tis faith disarms destruction.
Believe, and taste the pleasures of a God!
Believe, and look with triumph on the grave.

In Memory of
CAPT ROBERT NEWMAN
who died March 23d 1806
Aged 51
Though Neptunes waves & Boreas blasts
Have tost me to and fro
Now well escaped from all their rage
I'm anchored here below
Safely I ride in triumph here
With many of our fleet
Till signals call to weigh again
Our Admiral Christ to meet
O may all those I've left behind
Be washed in Jesus' blood
And when they leave this world of sin
Be ever with the Lord

In Memory of
BETSEY,
Wife of David Darling, died
March 23d, 1809,
JE. 43.
She was the mother of 17 children, and around
her lies 12 of them, and two were lost at sea.
BROTHER SEXTONS,
Please to leave a clear berth for me
near by this stone.

David Darling was a gravedigger at Copp's Hill when the stone was placed there for his wife, Betsey. He was also sexton of the North Church and lived on nearby Salem Street. He died in September 1820; he had requested that he be buried next to his wife upon his death, as indicated by the message on the stone. But David's request was ignored, and he was buried in some distance from his wife and family. There is no monument to David's memory anywhere in the graveyard.

The chipped and flaking old tombstones that stands under the trees at Copp's Hill have earned our respect and they continue to hold a fascination and connection to the roots of American history. Many of their stories have been lost to urban depravity, but when we remember them, we breathe life back into this old city of the dead.

SAGAMORE CEMETERY, BOURNE

When the grass shall cover me,
Holden close to earth's warm bosom, —
While I laugh, or weep, or sing,
Nevermore, for anything,
You will find in blade and blossom,
Sweet small voices, odorous,
Tender pleaders in my cause,
That shall speak me as I was —
When the grass grows over me.
When the grass shall cover me!

—Ina Coolbrith, "When the Grass Shall Cover Me"

You can't ignore the story of the ghosts in the Sagamore Cemetery, located on Route 6A in Bourne, Massachusetts, which is known as the gateway to Cape Cod. Bordered by Plymouth and Wareham, English colonists lived in Bourne as early as 1627. The burial ground is spacious and features a gnarly old tree that looks as though it has swallowed several bodies over the years, due to its eerily fascinating shapes. The stories of the ghosts that inhabit this graveyard have been in everything from the local papers to Boston television news broadcasts. The first burial recorded in the Sagamore Cemetery was in 1803, and most of the gravestones here date back to the nineteenth century.

There are many who reside here that were removed from the old Bournedale cemetery. Apparently, there was a bit of confusion when many of the bodies were being moved to their new resting place at Sagamore in new coffins built by Keith Car Works, a local manufacturer of box rail cars. Unfortunately, the wrong headstones were placed over some of the disinterred remains, leading to speculation as to the correct location of some of the bodies. The remains of the Bournes themselves were part of the upheaval in the burial ground. Their graves were displaced to make way for construction of the Cape Cod Canal. The family included Capt. Elisha Bourne (1733–1804) who was banished as a Tory to Rhode Island during the Revolutionary War. Captain Bourne was only allowed to return home under an act of the Legislature. After Captain Bourne passed away, his body was also buried in the Sagamore cemetery, which was quickly becoming the resting place for many of the prominent families of the area. The mixup of the moved remains has only contributed to the ghost stories that are told by the local residents.

The burial ground is the final resting place of Isaac Keith, a local businessman who reportedly has haunted the grounds for many years. Some folks think that Keith might be disturbed because of the grave mix-up. The cemetery is an attraction for paranormal investigators, psychics, and ghost tours. The psychics believe that the spirit of Capt. Elisha Bourne is disturbed about the misplaced graves. There have been several accounts of people who have felt an icy-cold grip enveloping around their bodies. Many visitors have seen a man in a top hat wandering through the cemetery, disappearing whenever approached, and others have claimed to have captured strange images of bright orbs and shadowy figures on camera.

There is an interesting story about a large marble gravestone found completely off of its foundation, with no logical explanation. Donald Ellis, the caretaker, was so disturbed by the moved stone that he called the police. But there was no evidence of vandals or pry marks, and Ellis and the police gave up trying to figure it out.

Another story involves Emory Ellis (no relation to Donald Ellis, the caretaker), a big cigar-smoking man who lived in the early part of the twentieth century. His family had a plot in the Sagamore Cemetery that was in the path of new construction. State officials ordered that the plot and it's inhabitants be moved, but Emory would have none of it, and kept the men at bay with a shovel and a shotgun when the state tried to move the burial ground. Eventually, he was offered enough money that he backed down and allowed his ancestors to be moved elsewhere on the grounds. But to this day, the smell of cigar smoke is prevalent in the cemetery, and some believe old Emory's spirit is still upset about his ancestors remains being moved.

Local ghost tours bring thrill seekers to the Sagamore cemetery hoping to catch a glimpse of the ghosts of the past. Visitors have run out of the cemetery claiming to have sensed an unseen presence walking behind them.

OLD BURIAL HILL, MARBLEHEAD

Almost all the old houses still stick to their rocks, and the streets are the same; where the
dead in Burial Hill to clamber out of the rocky niches where they sleep
within sound of the sea they loved, they would have little trouble finding
their old homes.
—*Hildegard Hawthorne,* Old Seaport Towns of New England

Located eighteen miles north of Boston, Massachusetts, is the quaint old town of Marblehead, Massachusetts. This scenic peninsula situated at the southeastern corner of Essex County boasts one of the most beautiful harbors on the North Shore. Officially founded in 1629, the narrow, picturesque streets are crowded with an amazing assortment of historic seventeenth- and eighteenth-century buildings. Originally inhabited by the Naumkeag Indians, remains of Native American villages, burial grounds, shell mounds, and even an Indian fort have been discovered over the years. Additional evidence such as spears, arrowheads, clubs, and a variety of utensils have been found scattered throughout Marblehead. The Naumkeag were a tall, strong-limbed people whose only article of clothing was a beast skin thrown over one shoulder, and another about the waist. Excavations along Atlantic Avenue in the late 1700s and into the 1800s indicate the former location of wigwams. Such an excavation in a field during November 1874, close to Salem Harbor, revealed a grave containing five skeletons— four adults, and one child. Amazingly, the skeletons were all well preserved, except for the child. The bodies were described as being

---

*–Granddaughter of celebrated writer, Nathaniel Hawthorne.

buried on their backs, facing west, except for one that faced east with the legs bent, and knees drawn up tightly against the chest, suggesting a traditional Indian burial. Besides the skeletons, the graves also contained other items, such as an earthen cup, a small bell, two seashells, and a number of beads. This additional discovery of these artifacts confirmed that the bodies were buried after the white settlers came to America.

In 1638, at the site of Marblehead's first meetinghouse, Burial Hill was founded. Overlooking Marblehead Harbor with a commanding view of the Atlantic Ocean, this high point in town is the final resting place of hundreds of Marblehead's first citizens and an estimated six hundred Revolutionary soldiers. (Of those soldiers' graves in the cemetery, only a very few of them are actually marked.) Accessible from an entrance on Orne Street and another from Pond Street, the burial ground looms large, sprawling out at the top of the granite-faced hill. The ancient slate tombstones lean towards every direction on the compass throughout the grounds. Gnarled trees with knotholes that seem more like black eyes stand sentinel throughout the cemetery. To look at pictures of the area taken over a hundred years ago, these twisting trees are but young branches reaching out from the ground. In their own way, the trees as well as the gravestones seem to help mark the passage of time here.

One of the most curious local legends is that of "Old Dimond," the wizard of Marblehead. Edward Dimond leased a large parcel of land for the sum of thirteen shillings yearly beginning in 1709. Old Dimond was said to have been able to conjure the power of the sea to do his bidding. Sea Captains from far and wide, as well as the townspeople, sought his mystical advice, for many believed in his great powers. Whether he got his power from the black arts or his booming voice alone, he was said to have the ability to bring distress upon his enemies and to help his friends avert disasters. Some people thought that his uncanny ability to foretell the future could shape their fortunes at sea.

On nights when waves crashed across Marblehead shores, the sky rumbled above, and the gale force winds blew, Old Dimond would make his way to Burial Hill while the townspeople hid safely in their homes. In between the tombstones of the cemetery, it was said that the wizard would "beat about" them while his voice echoed out over the waters. Clearly heard above the roar of any tempest were the powerful words of Old Dimond. He would command orders for the management and fate of the ships at sea. According to the tales about Old Dimond, no one would dare to question his ability to save someone from a shipwreck simply with his words. Dressed in an indigo cloak whirling about the tombstones in the middle of stormy nights, the wizard would spend hours in the cemetery controlling the forces of nature. It has been said that he would shriek to the sailing vessels, "Belay there and harken to the voice of Old Dimond."

One day a man had come to visit the wizard for advice; however, he was guilty of stealing wood from a poor old widow. Old Dimond was able to put a charm upon the robber that forced him to walk through town all night with a heavy load of wood on his back. According to local legend, Old Dimond was also able to help an old couple who had their money stolen from them by telling them where the money was hidden and who had taken it. Old Dimond's granddaughter, Moll Pitcher, carried on his magical legacy in neighboring Lynn, Massachusetts. Moll inspired poet John Greenleaf Whittier to write about her in a piece simply entitled "Moll Pitcher." A passage from the poem reads:

> Even she, our own weird heroine,
> Sole Pythoness of ancient Lynn,
> Sleeps calmly where the living laid her;
> And the wide realm of sorcery,
> Left, by its latest mistress, free,
> Hath found no gray and skilled invader

Nearly two hundred years later, tales of Old Dimond are still being told in and around Marblehead. It is said that on dark nights that the wizard's voice can still be heard yelling commands into the winds that cross Old Burial Hill. Others say that his indigo cloak can be seen moving between the stones, as if he had never left the hill.

Tales of apparitions include the legend of a man in town who was chased all night long by a corpse in a floating coffin, and shortly thereafter he became very ill and died. Another story is told about a young fisherman who arrived home late one night and met with the young woman to whom he was betrothed. He gave her some of the fish that he had caught, only to see her disappear right before his eyes. The next morning he learned that his fiancé had died while he was at sea. Heartbroken, he realized it was her ghost to whom he'd given the fish. What the apparition did with the fish has never been determined.

In the cemetery you can find the memorial stone that was placed there in 1998 by the town of Marblehead in remembrance of Wilmot Redd. Her small house was next to Old Burial Hill on the southeast corner of the pond that now bears her name. In 1692, in neighboring Salem Village, during the Salem witchcraft hysteria, Wilmot Redd was among those accused. She was described as a crusty old woman with a very sharp tongue who was most unpopular with the townspeople, especially the womenfolk. She was married to a fisherman, Samuel Redd, and the local fisherman knew her as "Mammy." Wilmot Redd was tried on September 17. She denied the charges, but was allowed no defense counsel. There was no one to speak on her behalf, including her husband. She was condemned to hang four days later on Gallows Hill. It is said that no one came to claim her body, and she ended up buried in an unmarked pauper's grave. Wilmot was the only Marblehead citizen executed for witchcraft.

Along the Minister's Row section of the burial ground is one of the most unique headstones in New England. The Susanna Jayne headstone was carved by Henry Christian Geyer, a prolific stone carver from Boston's South End, and it was commissioned by her husband Peter Jayne. The crown, or top of the stone, has an unusual shape, which is well protected in a granite encasement.

The symbolism on this stone is profound. There is an hourglass and bones, a reminder that our time on earth is fleeting. When our time is up, our bodies turn from bones to eventual dust. There are two smiling winged cherubs to represent the heavens, and two bats to represent hell. Encircling much of the carvings is a snake swallowing its own tail, creating a never-ending circle, also known as the Uroborus, a symbol of eternity. The scythe also represents death, and the divine harvest; much like the wheat that grows to maturity, the harvest is then reaped and taken. The skeleton holds the sun and the moon, depicting the cycle of life, and in some interpretations, the Old Testament and the New Testament. The skeleton wears a wreath of laurels and is wrapped in a cloak or cloth symbolizing victory over death, and the souls triumph over the trial of an earthbound existence. The epitaph reads:

Deposited
Beneath this Stone the Mortal Part
of Mrs. Susanna Jayne, the amiable Wife of
Mr. Peter Jayne, who lived Beloved
and Died Universally Lamented, on
August 8th 1776 in the 45th
Year of her Age.

"Precious in the Sight of the Lord is the Death of his Saints."

Here Sleeps the precious Dust — She Shines above,
Whose Form was harmony, whose soul was Love.
What were her Virtues? all that Heaven could Spare
What were her Graces? all Divinity Fair.
Mingling with Angels, they admire a Guest,
As spotless Good, and lovely as the Rest.

Located near the gazebo on Old Burial Hill is a monument to a tragic event. A fleet of ships from Marblehead was caught in a hurricane as they were fishing the Grand Banks of Newfoundland on September 19, 1846. Sixty-five men perished and at least eleven vessels were lost. The fishing industry in Marblehead never recovered from this horrific occurrence. In 1848, the "Fishermen's Monument" was dedicated by The Marblehead Charitable Seamen

Society. It lists the names of the deceased who were lost at sea. On this monument is the following inscription:

LOST
On the Grand Banks of Newfoundland
In the Memorable Gale of September 1846
65 Men and Boys
43 Heads of Families
155 Fatherless Children
"The Sea Shall Give Up the Dead That
Were In It."

Should you find the scene of the graveyard slightly familiar, you may recognize it from the movie, *Hocus Pocus*. This fictional, family-friendly Disney movie filmed in the area in 1993 is about the three Sanderson sisters who were seventeenth-century witches that were conjured up by unsuspecting pranksters in present-day Salem. The daytime graveyard scene was filmed at Old Burial Hill.

The hours spent wandering this burial ground can pass so quickly with the large amount of ornate and unique carvings to see. Should you dare to stay around after sunset, you may find the wind carrying the smell of the ocean and the bellowing voice of Old Dimond. In between the long shadows of the tombstones as the night shades the cemetery in a dark cover, look closely for the indigo cloak weaving amongst the stones.

Pentucket Burial Ground, Haverhill

Our vales are sweet with fern and rose,
Our hills are maple-crowned;
But not from them our fathers chose
The village burying-ground
With scanty grace from Nature's hand,
And none from that of Art.
A winding wall of mossy stone,
Frost-flung and broken, lines
A lonesome acre thinly grown
With grass and wandering vines.
Without the wall a birch-tree shows
Its drooped and tasselled head;
Within, a stag-horned sumach grows.
Fern-leafed, with spikes of red.
There, sheep that graze the neighborly plain
Like white ghosts come and go,
The farm-horse drags his fetlock chain,
The cow-bell tinkles slow.
Low moans the river from its bed,
The distant pines reply;
Like mourners shrinking from the dead,
They stand apart and sigh.
Unshaded smites the summer sun,
Unchecked the winter blast ;
The school-girl learns the place to shun,
With glances backward cast.

—John Greenleaf Whittier, "The Old Burying-Ground"

Originally established as Pentucket in taking its name from the Pentucket Indian tribe, the meaning of Pentucket was the "land of the winding river," as the Merrimack River weaves through the southern part of the city. The land was sold by two sachems, or Indian Chiefs, Passaquoi and Saggahew, to the colonists for the sum of three pounds and ten shillings. The deed was signed by six colonists, and the two natives signed each with a drawn image of a bow and arrow. Haverhill was named after the birthplace of one of the settlement's first ministers, John Ward, in England.

Haverhill is part of Essex country bordering New Hampshire, and boasts a fascinating old burial ground that was begun around the 1660s. The village was quickly organized with the building of the meetinghouse, and the establishment of roads, the raising of barns, and the planting of apple orchards. In the winter of 1697, there was a horrifying attack by Indians on the village. Mr. Sewell, one of the villagers, wrote of the incident, "They came as they were wont, arrayed with all the terrors of a savage war-dress, with their muskets charged for the contest, their tomahawks drawn for the slaughter, and their scalping knives unsheathed and glittering in the sunbeams." Six homes were burned to the ground, and at least thirty-nine people were killed or captured in the confrontation.

It was during that raid that Hannah Dustin became famous for her bravery and survival skills. The Indians brutally killed Hannah's six-day-old child by smashing the baby's skull against a tree. While Hannah's husband managed to escape the attack, she, along with her midwife, Mary Neff, were captured by the Indians and they were forced to march in the freezing cold 150 miles towards Canada through the New Hampshire wilderness. Hannah and Mary soon met another captive of the Indians, a fourteen-year-old boy by the name of Samuel Lennardson, who had been kept prisoner by the Indians for nearly one year. In the dark cover of night, Hannah planned her revenge and escape. In a daring ambush, Hannah struck with a vengeance by killing her captors—two men, two women and six children—on a small island along the Contoocook River. With a hatchet, she scalped her victims, and only one woman and a young man escaped the attack. Hannah, Mary, and Samuel fled in a canoe down the Merrimack River.

The scalps were presented in the General Court in Boston where they received a total of fifty pounds as a bounty. There is a bit of debate about Hannah's capture and revenge. Some people think that she is a hero, while others describe her as a villain. There is a statue that was placed in her memory in Haverhill, and another statue on the small island where the incident took place, just outside of Boscawen, New Hampshire. It is believed that Hannah is buried in an unmarked grave in the Pentucket Burial Ground. On Sunday, August 29, 1708, Haverhill was attacked by over one hundred French and Indians. Nearly forty people were killed and many others were taken captive. Homes were destroyed and once again the town was burned. Many victims of the second attack are buried in unmarked graves in the south end of the burial ground.

In 1736, the throat distemper was rampant in Haverhill. Most of the victims were children, and the affliction sent nearly one-quarter of the population (under the age of fifteen) swiftly into their graves. There were accounts that nearly every household was grieving from their losses due to the distemper epidemic, and funerals were a daily occurrence. Many children awoke in the morning as the picture of perfect health, but as soon as the night crept in, the children were laid down cold and silent in what was called the "winding sheet of the dead." Records from this time state that 58 families lost 1 child each; 34 families lost 2 each; 11 families lost 3 each; 5 families lost 4 each, and 4 families lost 5 each. Only one person died with this disease that was over forty years of age.

The affliction was described as a sore throat, white or ash-colored specks, translucent skin, and then the entire body would shut down. Also known as the "plague in the throat," it was described as a form of strangulation of the affected person in a very short time. There are numerous graves for children in this peaceful burial ground.

There is an amazing tree in the center of Pentucket Burial Ground, and it truly does appear to be the quintessential spooky tree. This tree doesn't offer a lot of leaves; in fact, there are numerous branches that are broken off, adding to its sinister appearance.

However, if this tree is not eerie enough, perhaps what resides in it will give you a shudder. The tree serves as a roosting ground for a colony of turkey vultures. The turkey vulture is a scavenger, and feasts almost entirely on carrion, the carcasses of dead animals. The turkey vulture finds its meals using its sense of smell, flying low enough to detect mercaptan, which is a gas produced by the process of decay in dead animals. The turkey vulture's head is bald and red, giving it a frightening look. This baldness is beneficial because the bird must stick its head inside the decaying carcasses to reach the meat. Their prehistoric appearance is enough to startle anyone. As they fly overhead, their long shadows move ominously across the burial ground.

A variety of crude fieldstone markers carved in the seventeenth century are evident throughout the burial ground. Some of these primitive stones exhibit simple faces, circular eyes, and pinwheels. The epitaphs read like a history book:

Abigail Codman
Consort of
Mr John Codman and
Daut of Capt John & Mrs Dorcas
Soley Who Departed this Life
In full Expectation of a better
Through a Redeemer
Sept The 4th 1775 Aged 51 Years
She was drove from Charlestown in
April 1775 by ye Cruel hand of Oppression.

In 1774, during the period of the American Revolution, Abigail's husband, Capt. John Codman, helped set ablaze British tea in the Charlestown, Massachusetts, public market. In response, the British burned down his home along with the rest of Charlestown.

There are abundant ghost stories in this old burial ground. An obelisk serves as a memorial for the devastating Indian attack of 1708. Visitors have remarked that the area around this monument emanates a tremendous amount of "psychic energy," while others describe a sensation of being watched or feeling a spirit presence. Electromagnetic frequency readers have detected erratic and unexplainable energy surges throughout the grounds. One of the local legends tells of an apparition on a horse riding among the graves during the darkest hours of the night.

The burial ground, with all of its inherent energy, seems to invite those who are interested in "dowsing." Dowsing with a pendulum, rods, or another instrument is a type of divination—an attempt to build a psychic connection established between the dowser and the sought-after object or spirit. The theory behind dowsing is that all things possess an energy force. The dowser, by concentrating on tuning in with these forces, can move dowsing rods or pendulums.

The opportunity to connect with the spirits of the past in Haverhill's Pentucket Burial ground invites ghost hunters and graveyard enthusiasts alike to this historic place full of captivating stories.

OLD DEERFIELD BURIAL GROUND, DEERFIELD

What of the Darkness? Is it very fair?
Are there great calms? And find we silence there?
Like soft-shut lilies, all your faces glow
With some strange peace our faces never know,
With some strange faith our faces never dare, —
Dwells it in Darkness? Do you find it there?

—Richard Le Gattienne, "What of the Darkness"

It is said that part of living life is the burial of the dead. Located in picturesque western Massachusetts is the village of Old Deerfield. First settled by European colonists in 1673, this settlement is a collection of eighteenth- and nineteenth-century houses filled with relics of hearth and home that reveal the intimate details of life in early New England. When English traders first arrived in what is now Deerfield in the 1640s, it was inhabited by the Pocumtucks, a small but prosperous and powerful group of Indians who had lived, farmed, fished, and hunted in the area for several generations.

At the beginning of the eighteenth century, Deerfield was one of a few settlements in western New England. On a cold winter morning in February 1704, 340 French and Indians swarmed over the frozen snow and raided the settlement. One hundred and twelve Deerfield men, women, and children were captured and taken on a three hundred-mile death march to Montreal, Canada, in harsh winter conditions. The ordeal through the snow, as deep as three feet, claimed many lives. Some people starved to death and others who couldn't keep up were hacked to pieces. Some of the captives were later redeemed and returned to Deerfield, but one-third chose to remain among their French and Native captors. Many of the Deerfield villagers were sold by the Indians to the French, who later ransomed them back to the British.

Deerfield was resettled in 1707 under the leadership of the town's first minister, Reverend John Williams. Reverend Williams had managed to survive the raid of 1704 and the long march to Canada. In addition, the Reverend was a captive of the French for two years, and he had lost his wife and two of his children during that time. Eunice, the Reverend's third child, married a Mohawk, and chose to remain with the Indians and French until her death in 1785.

The stones in the old burial ground of Deerfield Village date back to the 1690s through the early 1800s, although it is believed that the site may have been a Native American burial ground at an earlier time. On the summit of a four-foot-tall grassy mound in the graveyard is a stone that is inscribed on one face: "The Dead of 1704," and on the opposite side, "The Grave of 48 Men Women and Children, victims of the French and Indian raid on Deerfield February 29, 1704". The marker was placed there in 1901, memorializing the mass grave for those who were killed in the Deerfield massacre.

In the collection of the Memorial Hall museum in Deerfield, there are some fascinating artifacts from the 1704 raid, including a door from what is known as the Old Indian House, which was also known as the Ensign John Sheldon House. The door retains the hole and gashes made by the French and Indian attackers. Also in the hall are marble tablets that describe the lives of many of those who were affected by the raid, and some that memorialize those who are buried in the old burial ground:

In honor of the Pioneers
of this Valley, by whose courage
and energy, faith and fortitude
the savage was expelled
and the wilderness subdued;
and to perpetuate the remembrance

of the sufferings at Deerfield,
FEB. 29, 1703–4,
when, before the break of day, 340 French and Indians,
under the Sieur Hertel de Rouville,
swarming in over the palisades on the drifted snow,
surprised and sacked the sleeping town,
and killed or captured
the greater part of its inhabitants.
On Tablets at either hand,
recorded in love and reverence by their kindred;
are the names and ages of those
who lost their lives in the assault,
or were slain on the meadows
in the heroic attempt to rescue the captives,
or who died on the hurried retreat to Canada,
victims to starvation

SARAH FIELD, 2.
MARY, her mother, 28,
Wife of JOHN,
With children,
MARY, 6, and JOHN, 3,
were captured.
Mary adopted by an Indian,
Was named WALAHOWEY.
She married a savage,
and became one.

Zechariah Field
1645–1674.
A settler at Pocumtuck
Before Philip's war.
His remains lie in an unknown grave
In the old burying ground.
Many of his descendants
Have attained international fame.

In his honor
This tablet is placed in 1903
by Marshall Field
of Chicago.

In Memory
of
Mr. Samuel Allen,
who was killed by the Indians on the meadow north of
The Bars Homestead
while valiantly defending his children,
August 25, 1746:
of Eunice Allen,
his daughter, aged 13, who was tomahawked by the Indians,
but survived:
of Samuel Allen,
his son, aged 8, who was taken captive by the Indians,
but after many months was rescued through the
gratitude of an Indian woman, by his uncle,
Col. John Hawks.
Both children thus restored to their mother,
Hannah Hawks Allen,
lived to be the oral historians of this eventful day
and of their generation.
Erected by the descendants of
Caleb Allen,
son of Mr. Samuel Allen of "The Bars".

This tranquil burial ground situated quietly behind Deerfield Academy offers several other stories. There is a dramatic carving on the gravestone for Mary Harvey. It was carved by Solomon Ashley, a misfit son of the minister, who had never married. Solomon had become a common potter and gravestone maker, and he eventually became a ward of the town. At the age of sixty-nine, he died by drowning.

Mary's husband was Simeon Harvey, the village blacksmith. Simeon was born in 1743 and was apprenticed to the trade in 1761 after a brief service in the army. In 1768, he married Mary, and one year later they had their first child. Every two years thereafter, another child was born into the family. However, in 1785, just five days before Christmas and just before Mary and Simeon's eighteenth wedding anniversary, Mary died giving birth to their tenth child. The gravestone for Mary is engraved with a simple carving of an open-faced coffin, with an image of Mary with her infant lying on her left arm, just as they were buried. This depiction of the deceased was quite unusual for the time.

Within the burial ground there are a variety of carvings including skulls and crossbones and curly haired angels. The stone for Abagail Williams, who died in 1754, features a rare design of a large clock with roman numerals, crossed bones, and a crossed shovel and pickax.

There are also several table stones in the burial ground that are about to crumble into the ground. In the early nineteen hundreds, it was said that the local boys used to use these tables to crack the nuts from the nearby trees, which may have contributed to the condition of these fragile stones.

Some of the grave markers that can be found are quite simple, without any ornamentation, such as the carving on a small red boulder that plainly reads, "Ma Dyed Novem 7 Anno 1696."

Other stones display the cause of death such as Smallpox in 1785, and a stone from 1793 reads, "As a tribute of gratitude to the memory of an indulgent stepmother." Another marker from 1804 offers this puzzling epitaph: "Your eyes are upon me, and I am not."

Another epitaph offers a story:

"On the 12th Day of May 1768, the Home of Mr. William Arms was Consumed by Fire And his Wife Mrs. Rebecca Arms unhappily perished in the Flames in the 70th year of her Age.

"She was one who Feared God & Lov'd the Redeemer, was a singular Example of Piety, who by a devout walk was a Bright Or name to the Christian Religion, And her Death Great Gain."

This burial ground offers a glimpse into the past of a small community of settlers who built a little village in the wilderness that was brutally attacked twice, and yet through perseverance they were able to carry on. Many people believe that the ghosts from the burial ground wander throughout the village and make appearances in the historic homes and buildings.

OLD BURIAL HILL, PLYMOUTH

*Plymouth harbor is a quiet place by moonlight,
and Burial Hill is a very quiet place. Yet it gave
us the most direct message we had — of spacious
thought dramatized in narrow setting, of definite
achievement with inadequate equipment, of the
resourceful valiance of those early people, and of
what Governor Bradford calls "their great patience
and allacritie (cheerful readiness) of spirit" in the face of life, and death.*

*—Frances Lester Warner, "Pilgrim Trails,"
from* The Atlantic Monthly, 1921

The stroll through Old Burial Hill in Plymouth, Massachusetts, is perhaps the most alluring in New England. With each step up the slanting stairs, you see more of them—twisting paths, shadowed trees, and then hundreds of tombstones, each one a reminder of a soul who passed through here lifetimes ago. Once you've reached the top, you get a fine view of the ocean beyond the rooftops of the downtown buildings. Sunlight filters through the trees creating twisted shadows on the stones, and moves slightly with every gentle breeze. The paths wind through the trees and down the sloping hillsides. The stones are so tightly crowded together that it would be nearly impossible to have one person standing in front of each stone comfortably. There almost doesn't seem to be enough room for everyone that is buried here. With the variety of carved facial expressions on the many portrait-style stones, one can't help but wonder if they are correct portrayals of those buried there.

The stories here are rich in American history, which is fitting given that the cemetery stands at the birthplace of America. The burial ground is 165 feet above sea level and was an early lookout post for the pilgrims. The first fort was built on the hill in 1622, then modified several times, and after approximately fifty years, the fort was abandoned. Sometime around the 1670s, the area was used for burial purposes. A majority of the older stones were British-made, and were shipped across the waters. The oldest surviving tombstone dates from 1681.

The stones here are a visual connection to some of the most fascinating stories from this old settlement. One of the most noticeable grave markers is that of Governor William Bradford. The over-eight-foot-tall marble obelisk marks the grave of the man who was elected Governor of Plymouth Colony thirty times. Born in Austerfield, Yorkshire, England, in March of 1588, he was the second signer and primary architect of the Mayflower Compact. He is also known as historian of Plymouth County, because of his 270-page journal, later named *History of the Plymouth Plantation* that chronicled the history of the Pilgrims and the original settlement in Plymouth. During the winter of 1656–1657, William Bradford was quite ill and on May 8, 1657, he predicted to his friends and family that he would die, and he did the next day at the age of sixty-nine. The inscription on the stone reads in part:

> Under this stone rest the ashes of William Bradford a zealous Puritan & sincere Christian Gov. of Ply. Col. from 1621 to 1657, (the year he died) aged 69, except 5 yrs. which he declined.

There is a small stone in remembrance of Caleb Cook, a soldier who killed the infamous King Philip. King Philip was a Wampanoag Indian leader who led an uprising against the New England colonists, which was known as King Philip's War. These raids were proportionately one of the bloodiest and costliest in the history of America. More than half of New England's ninety towns (including Deerfield, Haverhill, Northfield, Bridgewater, Scituate, and Northampton) were assaulted by Native American warriors in the seventeenth century. In battle at Providence, Rhode Island, Caleb's gun, after an initial misfire, shot King Philip directly in the heart. After the fatal shot, Caleb ran out of the bushes to exchange guns with him, as he desired to have the gun that King Philip carried. This gun was a treasured heirloom that was passed down in the Cook family for hundreds of years. King Philip's body was drawn and quartered; his limbs were hung from the trees, and his decapitated head was brought back to Plymouth where it was put on stake and displayed for over thirty years.

There is the local legend of a witch known as Mother Crewe who many believed was responsible for putting several people in their graves on Old Burial Hill. Mother Crewe was avoided by many people in town, whether or not they believed in witchcraft. She was thought to be responsible for causing plants and crops to rot on the vine with no explanation. Her spell craft was blamed for ships being driven ashore along the coast. There was even a story about her causing villagers to be stricken with smallpox.

There was an occasion where Plymouth resident Southland Howland rode up to Mother Crewe's door and attempted to seize her property, as he felt that he was the rightful owner. Howland demanded that she give up her home to him under the law of entail (a common law at that time that restricted the sale of property, protecting the inheritance of the heirs) as her home was in a desirable location. With a snap of his whip upon Mother Crewe's door, Southland laid claim to the property. When she stood firm and told him that he had no rights to the claim, he told her that he would "tear down" her cabin by the next Friday.

Angered by his threats, she responded, "On Friday they'll dig your grave on Burying Hill. I see the shadow closing round you. You draw it in with every breath. Quick! Home and make your peace!"

Undeterred, Southland replied, "Bandy no witch words with me, woman. On Friday I will return." With that he swung himself on to his horse into his saddle. All of a sudden a black cat jumped onto Mother Crewe's shoulder, hissing. Her anger raged, and she raised her hand and cried, "Your day is near its end. Repent!"

But Southland just reiterated his demands. "Bah! You have heard what I have said. If on Friday you are not elsewhere, I'll tear the timbers down and bury you in the ruins."

"Enough!" shrieked the hag, "My curse is on you here and hereafter. Die! Then go down to hell!" Mother Crewe's cat jumped on the horse, clawing at him, and the horse ran off wildly.

A sinister fog encircled the town and brought a cold gloom to the air. Just before dark, the dead body of Southward Howland was found lying on the ground, not far from Mother Crewe's house. Southland Howland's sudden death was unexplained and remains a mystery. Was it just happenstance that his corpse was buried Friday on Old Burial Hill?

The book, *Dr. Le Baron and His Daughters*, published in 1890 by Author Jane G. Austin, describes Mother Crewe commanding a curse:

> But mother Crewe's face showed no sign of relenting as she gazed upon that trembling figure, decked out with its poor attempt at bridal finery; indeed, an added scorn and detestation seemed to gather upon her brow, and, bending over the girl, her arms stiffly extended upward, she deliberately cursed her in all the detail of anathema to be gathered from the black and bitter pages of wizard lore : sleeping, waking, in her home and among her neighbors, in her body and in her soul, in her life and in her death, and in a dishonored grave. " And may your husband fail in all he undertakes and die of a broken heart, and may all your sons be cripples, and all your girls lighted and deserted as mine has been, and no one to pity or to help."

In this book, the story of a young sailor named Ansel Ring, who was cursed by Mother Crewe, was revealed. Ansel was a sailor on the ill-fated, armed brigantine *General Arnold*, under the command of Captain James Magee of Boston in 1778. A terrible blizzard blew into Plymouth harbor the day after Christmas. Perilously in danger offshore, the ship dropped anchor and was hung up in an area known as White Flats, a treacherous sandbar just northwest of the breakwater.

Fierce waves pummeled the ship and the bitter winter temperatures dropped below zero. Captain Magee told the crewmen to put rum in their shoes to ward off frostbite, but many drank it instead, dying quickly thereafter. In a blinding snowstorm, the crew desperately tried to survive the night; their screams through the wailing winds could be heard in the settlement from across the water. The frosty morning light revealed seventy-two exposed bodies, frozen to death and strewn about the ship. Doctor Thatcher, a Plymouth native, viewed the horrible discovery and chronicled the account:

> Seventy dead bodies, frozen into all imaginable postures, were strewed over the deck, or attached to the shrouds and spars; about thirty exhibited signs of life, but were unconscious whether in life or death. The bodies remained in the posture in which they died; the features dreadfully distorted. Some were erect, some bending forward, some sitting with the head resting on the knees, and some with both arms extended, clinging to spars or some parts of the vessel.

The dead were piled on the floor of the Court House, and it is said that Dr. Robbins fainted when called to perform the religious services.

On Burial Hill a mass grave was dug for those who died on the ship. There was no complete list of names of those onboard. Many of the voyagers had been picked up in Boston, before the brig set sail south, and they hadn't been on board long enough for the captain to log their identities. The tragedy cast a dark shadow on Plymouth that year. The townspeople who witnessed the horrific scene, who heard the screams, wanted to forget, but couldn't. Years passed, and somehow the weight of time buried the tale on Old Burial Hill. Alongside one of the many pathways in the burial ground is the monument that serves as a reminder of those dark days in 1778. Buried on the hill is Ansel Ring, who froze to death on the ship.

There is a stone on the hill marking the grave of Hannah Howland who died "of a Languishment" on January 25, 1780. Hannah is said to have died of a broken heart because of the passing her lover, Ansel. Perhaps Mother Crewe's curse had come to pass.

The monument marking the grave of the sailors of the brigantine General Arnold can be found at the far edge of the burial ground, near the Russell Street parking lot. The inscription on the northeasterly side is:

In memory of Seventy two Seamen who perished in
Plymouth harbour
on the 26, and 27, days of December 1778,
on board the private armed Brig, Gen. Arnold, of twenty guns,
James Magee of Boston, Commander, sixty of whom were buried
on this spot.

On the northwesterly side:

Capt. James Magee died in Roxbury, February 4, 1801;
aged 51 years.

On the southwesterly side:

Oh! Falsely flattering were yon billows smooth
When forth, elated, sailed in evil hour,
That vessel whose disastrous fate, when told,
Fill'd every breast with sorrow and each eye
With piteous tears.

On the southeasterly side:

This monument marks the resting place of sixty of the
seventy two mariners,
"who perished in their strife with the storm,"

and is erected by Stephen Gale of Portland, Maine, a stranger to
them, as a just memorial of their sufferings and death.

There are numerous tales from the locals who claim to see the
image of the brigantine *General Arnold*, and they describe it as a
phantom ship that sails the harbor, almost like a mirage.

Throughout the cemetery are stones that tell a variety of
stories. Numerous stones for shipwrecks and those lost at sea can
be found with remarkable carvings. There is the gravestone for
Captain Chandler Holmes who died October 4, 1831, at the age of
twenty-seven. The image depicts a sinking ship in the ocean with
a trumpeting angel flying above. There is the grave for Richard
Holmes, who was drowned in the Pacific Ocean and died near the
port of Lima (Peru) at the age of twenty-two. This dramatic carving
reveals an angel trumpeting over a floating coffin. The image of
another carving depicts a tragedy at sea. Lightning, bands of rain,
and waves washing over a ship's decks can be seen on the stone for
Joseph Churchill, who died at fifty-four. The epitaph reveals the
ill-fated voyage of the brigantine *Plymouth Rock* in November 1836
bound to Rochelle in France that foundered at sea. The same stone
conveys the story of his son who also met a watery fate: Captain
Joseph Lewis of Portland, Maine, at the age of thirty-seven, died on
the brigantine Androscoggin in August 1842.

There are quite a large number of portrait stones throughout the
burial ground. Some of the carvings for women depict them being
adorned with necklaces that have hearts on them. A fascinating
carving for Nathaniel Morton depicts a well-dressed man rising
from behind a grave marked with two skulls and crossbones.

The Hill itself is not without its ghostly legends as well. With all
of the fantastic carvings and tragic tales, it's not surprising that the
spirits are active. Visitors to the burial ground have claimed to have
seen shadow people wandering the grounds, sometimes walking
between the trees as if the ghosts of the past were still keeping watch.
There is an unsettling story of a group of five people who wandered
between the stones on a gloomy November evening. While the
group stopped to talk, they heard loud footsteps coming up the

sidewalk directly towards them. The group frantically searched for the source of the sound, but found nothing. They quickly found the nearest exit and made a hasty retreat, in complete disbelief of what had transpired. Tour groups regularly walk the well-trodden paths, and stories have been told of cameras capturing mysterious light anomalies, orbs, and other unexplainable phenomena. There's a building close to the cemetery that is rumored to be haunted as well. The top floor was used by medical students who dissected fresh bodies obtained from Burial Hill.

Another noteworthy burial site in town is on Cole's Hill, which affords a sweeping view of the bay into which the Mayflower sailed and the shore on which its passengers landed. At the foot of Cole's Hill is Plymouth Rock, legendary landing site of the Pilgrims and steppingstone to the New World. On the hill there is a statue of Massasoit that reads, "Great Sachem of The Wampanoags Protector and Preserver of the Pilgrims 1621, Erected by the Improved Order of Red Men as a Grateful Tribute 1921."

Nearby is a sarcophagus, which contains the bones of the pilgrims that have been found at various times near its location. It was erected by the General Society of Mayflower Descendants in 1920. A part of the inscription reads, "The Monument marks the First Burying Ground in Plymouth of the passengers of the Mayflower. Here under cover of darkness the fast dwindling company laid their dead, leveling the earth above them lest the Indians should know how many were the graves."

There are numerous accounts of this burial site being discovered in a rather grisly manner. In the book, *The Pilgrim Republic* by John A. Goodwin, published in 1879, the following is recounted:

> In a storm of 1735 a torrent pouring down Middle Street made a ravine in Cole's Hill and washed many human remains down into the harbor. In 1809 a skull with especially fine teeth was exposed. In 1855 these graves were exposed in laying the public conduit on Cole's Hill. In one grave lay two skeletons, pronounced by surgeons male and female. The man had a particularly noble forehead; and it was fondly surmised

that here were the remains of Mr. and Mrs. Carver. These found a new grave on Burial Hill; but the other relics, with barbaric taste, were placed in the top of the stone canopy over Forefathers' Rock. In 1879, during some work on the southeast side of the hill, many more bones were unearthed, and some, with questionable taste, were carried away by the spectators in remembrance of their "renowned sires."

Plymouth is a resting place for the brave men who settled this wild land, who suffered and struggled to shepherd the beginnings of what became a free nation. Perhaps their spirits look out over the hills of this deep-rooted town and still keep watch over the rolling waves of the bay.

OLD MEETINGHOUSE CEMETERY, PRINCETON

Lost lamb! There is a starry fold.
Where innocence is safe forever:
There chilling frosts and wintry cold
Find entrance never.
Far from this sphere of doubt and gloom
The folding arms of love are round thee;
With flowers of everlasting bloom
Have angels crowned thee.
Sweet, perished bud of promise rare!
Through cloud-rifts in the gloom impending.
Streams light to comfort our despair,
The darkness rending.
Safe from the troubles that molest
Earth's pilgrim toward the sunset hieing,
On the good Shepherd's tender breast
Our lamb is lying.
If earnest prayer could bring him back,
I would not plead for his returning,
Where dimly, in the midnight black,
Hope's star is burning — 'Where Sorrow, with a trembling hand,
The death-dimmed eye of Beauty closes,
And Love goes mourning, through the land,
For her lost roses.

—W.H.C. Hosmer, "The Lost Lamb"

A winding road alongside Mount Wachusett brings us to the Old Meetinghouse burial ground in Princeton, Massachusetts, and a truly tragic tale. The mystery surrounding the disappearance of little Lucy Keyes has been debated and discussed for generations in this town. Robert Keyes purchased nearly two hundred acres of property at the foot of Wachusett Mountain in 1751, and his was one of the first five families to settle in the area. A blacksmith by trade, Robert soon became a skilled huntsman in this very wild and unsettled land. His house was built near what was known as the old Indian trail. There were ten children born into in the Keyes family. On April 14, 1755, Lucy Keyes, aged four years and eight months, went with her two sisters into the woods for about a mile's walk towards Wachusett Lake to bring back some sand for the house. In the shadows of the woods, Lucy wandered away from her sisters and became lost. Every able body for nearly thirty miles around Princeton was gathered to search for Lucy. Trudging through the forest for days and weeks, no evidence of Lucy could be found. Efforts were even made to drag the pond numerous times for any sign of the little girl. All of their pursuits and efforts were in vain—Lucy Keyes was never found. Lucy's mother, Martha, refused to give up hope, and she would venture into the woods for hours crying "Lucy, Luuucy." Many townspeople thought that she had been driven to the verge of insanity in her desperate search for her lost child. Adding further to the emotional upheaval were rumors that began to circulate of Lucy being taken captive by the Indians.

Ten years after Lucy's disappearance, her father petitioned the General Court of the Province of Massachusetts for support. He explained his family's desperate and costly efforts to find Lucy, and requested assistance as he was finding it difficult to afford the maintenance of his home and land. The petition was rejected and he ended up selling most of his property just to survive. Mrs. Martha Keyes died August 9, 1789, and her husband died March 1, 1795. They are both buried in the old Meetinghouse Burial Ground.

Shortly after the deaths of Martha and Robert, two men from Groton, Massachusetts, returned from a trip to Canada and claimed to have met a white woman there who matched Lucy's description. They stated that she knew nothing of her name or family, only that she lived near 'Chusett Hill.

Even stranger than the Indian story was a letter that was found describing, in gruesome detail, the murder of little Lucy Keyes. The letter was from Tilly Littlejohn, and was believed to have been written on his deathbed. Tilly claimed to be Keyes's neighbor, who had gotten into a bitter dispute with Robert Keyes over the boundaries of their property lines. A heated argument had ensued and Tilly sought his revenge when he found Lucy in the woods. He confessed to killing her by hitting her head on a fallen tree. He then stuffed her body inside a hollow log and waited until nightfall to dig a hole and bury the body at the base of an uprooted tree. As the search party continued to look for Lucy, they had found a lock of hair in the vicinity of where he said he had killed Lucy. The family had identified the hair as Lucy's, and Tilly became nervous that the murder might be uncovered, so he decided to leave the area soon after. There were questions about parts of the strange letter, as some facts did not seem to add up, creating even more confusion and speculation to Lucy's disappearance.

The grave for Martha Keyes is easily found in the cemetery and is often decorated with tokens of remembrance. Beads, pennies, ribbon, even a little ceramic lamb are some of the mementos left by those who still acknowledge Martha's pain and never-ending mourning for her lost child. With the numerous sightings and encounters with Martha's spirit, the story of little lost Lucy is frequently recalled. Visitors to the cemetery have claimed to hear a woman's voice on the wind calling, "Lucy, Lucy." An apparition of a woman dressed in colonial clothing is often seen wandering about the woods and cemetery.

During the shooting of a movie filmed for the Lifetime Channel based on the story of Lucy Keyes, there were numerous instances of unusual activity. Photographs revealed strange mists around the grave of Martha, and when reviewed by local paranormal groups, they were thought to show a portal or a doorway between our world and the spirit world. In some of these photos there was an image of a woman, which seemed to be passing through the worlds. Other photos show vapors and what is thought to be spiritual energy in the graveyard. One curious photo was described as an image of a man wearing a priest's cloak and a broad-brimmed hat standing with a book in his hands at the stone wall in the back of the cemetery.

Those who work at the nearby Wachusett Mountain ski area tell stories of hearing strange sounds and seeing unexplained shadows on the mountain. One tale describes seeing fresh child-size footprints in the snow at two o'clock in the morning, when no one else was around. The mystery and lore of Lucy Keyes's disappearance intrigues the Princeton Historical Society to this day. They have Lucy's cradle in their collection of antique artifacts, and they have documented the ghost stories from visitors to the mountain as well.

The peaceful atmosphere of this old burial ground is broken by a lingering sadness there, and one cannot help but be compelled to look into the adjacent woods and contemplate Lucy's fate. Does the spirit of Martha Keyes still tread the mossy grove of this burial ground? Are her plaintive cries still echoing in the woods? Some say one visit will make you a believer.

In addition to Martha's grave, there are a number of other interesting headstones in the burial ground, and many are worth noting. Two gravestones of interest mark the burials of Africans Thomas and Flova, who were "negro" servants interred there in 1783 and 1778, respectively. These stones feature unique carvings of faces with African features and hair. Most servants during this time period were buried in unmarked graves making these stones quite unusual.

Near the decrepit gate to the burial ground are two tombs, including the town tomb. The doors to them are missing and are now bricked shut. Small holes can be found in the crumbling brickwork that allows the morbidly curious a glimpse into the gloom of the crypt with a flashlight or camera. The tombs do not disappoint with bones strewn on the floor amidst deteriorating bricks. Strangely, there are no skulls to be found among the variety of dusty bones, surrounded by intricate cobwebs.

As the sun sets each day over this cemetery, the ghosts and the mysteries of the past slip further into the shadows of the trees on Wachusett Mountain. The mysterious disappearance of Lucy Keyes will remain forever unsolved in the darkness of Princeton, Massachusetts.

MAYFLOWER HILL
CEMETERY, TAUNTON

Far off the clocks are striking,
'Tis midnight's deepest shade,
The lamp but feebly glimmers, —
Thy little bed is made.
Around the house go mourning
The winds so drearily;
Within we sit in silence,
And listen, as for thee.
Dreaming that we shall hear thee
Knock softly at the door,
A weary with the wandering,
Glad to return once more.
Poor fools! thus to dissemble!
The fond hope will not stay;
We wake and feel too surely
Thy home is far away.

Eichendohff, "Midnight"

Astory that has evolved into somewhat of a local legend takes place in the Mayflower Hill Cemetery in Bristol County. This industrial city offers a beautiful garden-style cemetery close to the center of town. Within the cemetery is a large family monument that lists the death of Veva L. Johnson, "born 28 Oct 1880 and died 26 Apr 1884." The large family obelisk is easy to find because right next to it is a cement rocking chair that states, "Her vacant chair."

---

* A German poet from the nineteenth century.

According to legend, Veva's mother had scolded her and made Veva sit on a chair in the corner. Her mother then had to leave for the store and she instructed Veva not to leave the chair, as she expected her to sit there until she came back. The building caught fire while Veva's mother was out, and Veva died whilst inside.

However, upon researching the details of the Johnson family, there was no record of little Veva dying in a fire. The facts of the story were that she died in the neighboring town of Raynham at the age of 3 years, 5 months, and 25 days. It was recorded that she died from a spinal disease. It was further documented that she had a younger brother, Carl, who would have been about two years old at the time of Veva's death. Veva's mother passed away in 1898 at a young age from diabetes.

There is a bit of speculation as to if a mother would make a child, who suffers from a painful and debilitating spinal disease, sit in a chair while she was gone. But therein lies the intrigue in this story: over time the facts became blurred, so the search for the truth only leads to further conjecture.

But what of the fascinating grave marker, the rocking chair? The legend continues that occasionally little gifts and stuffed animals appear in the chair, and one can imagine the ghost of little Veva obediently sitting in the chair, playing with the toys.

It is important to note that although unusual in nature to find a stone chair in a burial ground, during Victorian times, this type of grave marker was just another way to reflect the imagery and customs at the time. Empty chairs and beds were symbols of the loss of a life, their presence being missed. There was even a superstition that if upon rising from a rocking chair, you left it rocking, it would be an omen of death. Rocking chairs also have a connection to children, as nurseries commonly have rocking chairs in them.

The chair will hold an intrigue for those with a ghostly imagination, but no matter, the legend of little Veva and her empty chair carries on in this stone city of the silent.

THE BODY SNATCHER OF
HAMPDEN COUNTY

I sought a grave a long forgotten grave
Neglected now some score of years or more once
I planted flowers and sought to save
The weeds and grass from rudely growing o'er
Twas in a public cemetery then
But thinly tenanted graves here and there this among a little
group was seen
Conspicuous by its florist's tender care now
I found that little grave plot grown
Into a crowded city of the dead tombstones thick as cottages were strewn
In lanes and alleys labyrinthine spread as I thread my way in solitude
Amidst that lonely crowd anxious to find stone
I sought musing in sadden'd mood
Of fleeting time and perishing mankind

—*John Hall, 1877,* A City of the Dead

A grisly tale of grave robbing comes from Springfield, Massachusetts, located in the scenic Pioneer Valley of western Massachusetts. These disturbing crimes took place from 1826 to 1830. The complete details were documented in a dusty old scrapbook that was kept in the city library, and were written by Dr. Alfred Booth, who was a reporter for the Republican newspaper, also out of Springfield. The account concerned the unorthodox practices of Doctor W.L. Loring. Dr. Loring was educated at Harvard Medical College, but despite a top-notch education he did not have a successful practice. Desperate for a solid source of income, Dr. Loring found an ambitious way to make fast money with some help from the dead.

The Pittsfield Medical College, in Pittsfield, Massachusetts, need bodies for dissection, but had limited opportunities to procure them. Dr. Loring undertook a scheme to supply the demand of the growing school by furnishing crematory remains, skeletons, and whenever possible, complete bodies.

On the morning of February 25th, 1826, in the cemetery at the foot of Elm Street, an empty grave sent a nervous chill throughout the community. Just a few days earlier Jonathan M. Moulthrop had hanged himself. Being a healthy person, his corpse was desirable for the doctors-in-training. According to the account in the newspaper, Moulthrop's body was discovered near the home of Dr. Loring by the armory, and while many people had suspicions that the doctor had removed the body from the grave there were no witnesses.

It wasn't long before the citizens became vigilant protectors of the recently deceased. Groups of people would hide out in the cemeteries, watching for anyone who looked suspicious. On one occasion, three young men watched over the grave of Mrs. Hamilton of Chicopee Falls. The men were concerned because Mrs. Hamilton had killed herself, with little damage done to her body. That night Dr. Loring and two of his students, Mr. Whitman, and Jacob Perkins, Jr., approached the grave, unaware that they were being watched until one of the spies shouted out, "What do you want there?" The Doctor feared that he might be caught and fled with his two accomplices. However, a few days later the doctor and his ghoulish henchmen visited the grave once again, and when they discovered that there was no one around, they stole Mrs. Hamilton's body.

After Mrs. Hamilton's corpse disappeared, the community became so alarmed some folks were reluctant to bury their dead, especially victims of suicide, since it was obvious Dr. Loring was targeting those poor souls. The family and friends of Mrs. Russell Curtis, another suicide, knew that her body would be a target and they decided not to bury her. Once the funeral at the old Methodist church on Union street, was over her body was removed and brought to the home of friends. Residents in the area described seeing three suspicious characters hovering around the house, and believed they were medical students from the Pittsfield school. Fearful that the body would be stolen, Mrs. Curtis's body was moved again after the second night. Her body was placed in the basement of the Methodist church, for what was simply described in the scrapbook as "a long time." The final resting place of Mrs. Curtis's body is unknown.

Another grave was robbed from the Elm Street cemetery. The body of William Nevers had disappeared. There was such an outcry at this point that the matter came before the selectmen of Springfield. An investigation followed, and Dr. Loring, Jacob Perkins, Jr., and George Ball were finally arrested. William Nevers body had been found in Westfield before it could be transferred to Pittsfield. After the arrests it was then decided that a tomb should be built for protection of the dead.

Dr. Loring's trial took place in May, 1819. Residents of the community waited anxiously to hear what his fate would be. Perkins was fined just fifty dollars and Dr. Loring was fined five hundred dollars. The Governor's Council felt that Dr. Loring's work was not "wholly unworthy."

After the trial, residents were still suspicious of Dr. Loring and they continued to blame him for strange occurrences over the next couple of years. A thirteen-year-old girl living near the city park in West Springfield said that she was awakened at 1:00 a.m. and found herself in the arms of a strange man who was carrying her from her bedroom through the back part of the house around to the outside gate of the yard. When she came to her senses, she struggled and jumped from the stranger's arms. The stranger then attempted to strangle her to silence her screams. Then, suddenly he dropped her, and she managed to run back to the house. When she ran inside she found her father preparing to pursue the invader. Despite the fact that everyone awoke that night and combed through the neighborhood searching for the girl's attacker, he was never found. An investigation ensued and three persons were brought before the girl for identification, one of whom was Dr. Loring. She selected him from the others as the guilty one, yet she could not be positive on this point and did not make the statement with absolute certainty of truth.

A young boy living in Wilbraham was so frightened that he might be abducted that every night in winter he poured water around the window casings and sash, so that the ice would prevent the doctor from opening the windows and carrying her away.

The doctor's reputation finally destroyed his practice and his family slid into poverty. His wife was treated sympathetically by the women in town, who believed that she was a woman of many good qualities. According to the reports about her, it was said that she had often been compelled to sleep in a bed with dead bodies hidden underneath. Eventually the doctor disappeared out of the area, leaving his wife and three children behind. She later married a clergyman and her family moved to another part of the country. It is unknown how many empty graves there are in Hampden County because of Dr. Loring and his henchmen.

There were specific quotes by Dr. Alfred Booth about Dr. Loring in the scrapbook:

"An anatomist who with all his Band of rude disciples over the subject hung And impolitely hewed his way through bones And muscles of the sacred human form Exposing barbarously to wanton gaze the mysteries of nature. Chill penury repressed his noble rage, And froze the genial current of his soul."

NEW HAMPSHIRE

PHILLIPS CEMETERY, JAFFREY

If life be as a flame that death doth kill,
Burn, little candle, lit for me,
With a pure flame, that I may rightly see
To word my song, and utterly
God's plan fulfill.

—*Charles Warren Stoddard, "A Rhyme of Life"*

A beautiful woodland cemetery can be found in the hills of Jaffrey, New Hampshire, in the vicinity of Mount Monadnock. A peaceful place with abundant wildlife, this burial ground can be a little challenging to drive up to, but it's worth the trip. Turn off of Mountain Road on to Fitzwilliam Road, and you will see the small white sign that reads Phillips Cemetery and the Phillips-Heil Cemetery. There doesn't seem to be a burial ground anywhere in sight, but a turn just before the sign down a dirt road with a short, challenging hill will bring you there. Surrounded entirely by tall trees, it seems to be an unusual place for a cemetery. There are more than one hundred graves in the burial ground, mostly dating from the nineteenth century. The ground is completely covered in a thick carpet of moss, which makes any footsteps in the cemetery just a little softer. What you will hear in the graveyard is the abundance of wildlife flying in and out of the woods and rustling in the trees around the stone walls.

This old burial ground was established by Lt. Governor Samuel Phillips in 1797. His son, Samuel Phillips, Jr., was the founder of Philllips Academy located in Andover, Massachusetts, which was founded in 1778. He also operated a gunpowder mill to provide General George Washington's troops with ammunition for the

Revolutionary War. The cemetery contains the remains of many of the original settlers, including the town founders who cleared the land in the late eighteenth century.

The dirt road continues alongside the burial ground and is a pleasant walk. Along the side of the road, surrounding one of the trees, is a curious circular stone wall. The road then leads to a very small, but modern cemetery with about fifteen graves. The lichen-covered trees that are throughout the grounds add a distinctive character to the location.

There is a family plot towards the far end of the burial ground, which is made quite obvious because of the life-size granite chair in the plot. These are the graves of the Ross family—four adults and two children. Each stone has a beautiful carving, and the one for little Jonas Ross, who died in 1812 at nine months, features the portrait of a little boy in a circle. The tombstones for the remaining family members are each unique in their own right. The imagery on the other stones includes a lily, a Celtic style cross, a broken rose, and a broken flower bud, which was appropriate because each died so young. With the exception of the elder Jonas, none of the family lived past the age of twenty-eight. Jonas Ross lived to be seventy-seven, passing away in 1861. His stone features a hand pointing skyward with the simple statement that, "God Is Love." The inscription on the stone chair reads "J. Ross" and the date of 1871.

The Ross family lived in the Jaffrey area for at least three generations. The fascinating legend about the chair relates to the ghosts of the past. A spiritual-minded descendant of the Ross family believed that deceased souls returned to the spot of their former existence. He had the chair placed next to the graves so their spirits could sit facing the sunset and reflect on their existence on earth. The stone chair is quite inviting for the living, and sitting in the shadow of the trees, it is easy to believe that not only are you communing with the peaceful nature around you, but with the spirits of the deceased as well.

POINT OF GRAVES, PORTSMOUTH

I'd like to walk around such hallowed ground,
Where friends we love await the Archangel's sound,
Within its precincts, holy thoughts arise—
To lead the spirit to its native skies.
The epitaphs engraven on each tomb
Disperse entirely every trace of gloom ;
Where Spring's sweet flow'rets sprouting 'neath
the feet, Comfort the mourner, and a fragrance give.

—"Sunbeams"

Located along the scenic Portsmouth, New Hampshire, waterfront is one of the most intriguing and haunted burial grounds along the seacoast. The gravestone carvings in this ancient burial ground rival any cemetery found in Boston, Massachusetts, as there are an amazing number of seventeenth century stones that still exist. These finely detailed stones with their grinning skeletons and sublime angels are waiting to tell their stories and are worthy of appreciation and acknowledgement. Many notable people are buried here, such as Captain Tobias Lear, father to the Secretary of George Washington, and Samuel Wentworth, father of Lieutenant Governor John Wentworth.

Portsmouth is one of the oldest settlements in America and was originally founded in 1623 as Strawberry Banke, named after the wild strawberries that grew along the shore. The Point of Graves burial ground was established in approximately 1671 and is the oldest known marked burial ground in the state. Deeded to the town by Captain John Pickering, the cemetery itself is only about an acre in size, but the stories seem to surpass that and one can easily become lost in time visiting the Point of Graves. The tall pines that border this quiet cemetery seem to speak with every ocean breeze and their shapes create long shadows that lead to the rows of leaning tombstones.

The name, "Point of Graves," comes from the fact that this burial ground was once surrounded on two sides by the Piscataqua River and took its name from the point of land on which it is situated. Eventually portions of the river were filled in, and the land was no longer on a prominent point. The neighboring ship wharves and warehouses were removed and the adjacent area was made into public gardens in the early twentieth century. The Prescott Park gardens add to the beauty of the waterfront but placed the river farther away from small the burial ground. Today it is nestled in a little corner on a side street that leads out to Pierce Island.

The oldest existing stone in the burial ground dates from 1683, however, it was written that burials of the Pickering family took place here before 1671. Early cemetery records are fairly scarce in Portsmouth, so there is no way to know exactly how old the burial ground is. In the late nineteenth century it was known as the ancient burying ground, and interments ended during this time due to overcrowding.

There is a curious entrance to the burial ground that not only offers a groaning swing gate as a portal, but also an iron turnstile. This turnstile is a rarity in New England cemeteries, but there was an important reason for its installation. When Captain Pickering gave the land to the town, he neglected to tell the town that he would allow his animals, horses, and cattle to graze on the property even after burials began. The turnstile was designed to keep the animals out and allow the visitors in. The land here is sloping and very uneven, due in part to the roaming animals during the early years.

Local writer and historian Thomas Bailey Aldrich once referred to the graveyard itself being dead—owing to its overgrown and abandoned condition. There were times when it was nearly impossible to walk the grounds because of the thistle barbs, tall grasses, and even wild strawberries that shrouded the stones. Currently, the burial ground is well maintained, the grass is neatly trimmed, and there is little to obstruct the views of the intricate gravestones. There are also several gravestones that have been repaired or restored in very recent years by the Portsmouth cemetery committee.

Every stone in the Point of Graves offers amazing artwork and detailed inscriptions and epitaphs to memorialize the dead. For example, one of the most ornate stones is for William Button, who died in 1693. At the age of thirty-seven, he was very successful and owned his own fleet of ships. However, he met his demise during a voyage along the Piscataqua River. William fell overboard from one of his own ships into the strong currents of the river, and when he was pulled from the water, he was dead. Carved on the stone are two intricate angels, each detailed right down to their teeth and swooping hair. There is also a tiny hourglass and winged skull that could be easily missed without closer examination. Even a miniature pinwheel is carved on the stone representing the cycle of life. There are large fruits depicted along the sides of the stone, representing that he lived a very abundant life.

Besides the captivating stones there are numerous stories of ghosts in the burial ground. Over the years many visitors to the Point of Graves report that it is haunted. The spirits are said to be so active that one visit might make a person a believer. People hear footsteps walking behind them, when no one is there. There is a sense of a presence in the burial ground, watching as visitors wander among the stones. Certainly you might be inclined to think that you are being watched while surrounded by carvings of skulls with vacant eye sockets.

The excavation of the Vaughn tomb and subsequent resetting of the broken marble gravestone adds a fascinating chapter to the history of the Point of Graves. In the far western corner on a little rise of earth in the Point of Graves is the Vaughn tomb. An account in August of 1884 about the opening of the tomb brings to light one of the mysteries about what lies underneath the burial ground, unseen to the eye. The cemetery originally had underground tombs that were more ornate than could be imagined for such a simple burial ground. The area surrounding the site of the original Vaughn grave marker was flat and there was no indication of what was under the marker until the digging began. The tomb was revealed during the first day of the excavation, after the old Vaughn tablet was removed for the purpose of laying a new foundation for a proposed monument. The tablet, which is 6 feet 10 inches in length and 3 feet in width, originally lied on the ground horizontally at the western end of the tomb directly over the entrance. No one was sure how this entrance to the underground tomb could have been used with the heavy tablet over it and it was quite a mystery during excavation. The entrance to the tomb was 4 feet in height and included an archway 2 feet 6 inches in width. It was thought that perhaps there was a rough wooden frame and door to the tomb. The archway above the entrance had broken away over the years, even though it still did exist in pieces. Upon opening the vault, a variety of artifacts were discovered. In the spaces between the arches were found numerous pieces of broken crockery, earthenware, and oxidized tin ware, and even an old ball of India rubber. The arched tomb was constructed of brick masonry, and measured 8 feet 6 inches in length, 8 feet in width, and 5 feet from the floor to the crown of the arch. The human remains were discovered with all of the skulls intact and facing upward, and were near the entrance to the tomb. There were no remnants of any of the coffins except for the iron handles that were just piles of oxidized dust. Amazingly, although the tablet only lists four names, there were twenty-eight well-defined skulls, leg bones, and ribs removed from the tomb. Dr. Shannon of Portsmouth removed the remains to a neighboring building where he cleaned and classified the bones. They were classified as follows: full-grown adults, 21; Young adults, 4; Children between five and eight years, 2; and one infant. It was even noted that the some adult skulls contained full sets of "exceptional" teeth and showed no appearance of decay. The doctor then sifted through the pile of remains and skillfully re-formed a complete skeleton of one of the children. It was even written that some of the local physicians made unsuccessful attempts to obtain some of the skulls for "professional purposes." On August 20, 1884, all of the excavated remains were carefully placed in a new casket, covered with a box of pine, and replaced in the tomb. The entrance was permanently sealed with solid masonry of stone and cement and a new monument was placed above the tomb. Today the original marker is on top of this monument and still displays the splitting crack across it. The East side of the polished monument bears the following inscriptions:

WILLIAM VAUGHAN
Emigrated from England about 1660
Member of the Royal Council for N. H. 1680–1715
Major Commandant Provincial Forces.
Justice of the Court of Common Pleas 1680–1686
Chief Justice of the Superior Court 1708–1715
Died 1719
GEORGE VAUGHAN
Son of Wm. and Margaret Vaughan
Born April 13, 1676
Graduated at Harvard Coll. 1696
Justice of the Court of Common Pleas 1707–1715
Lt. Governor of New Hampshire 1715–1717
Died Dec. 1724
ELIZABETH, wife of Lt. Gov. GEORGE VAUGHAN
and daughter of Robert Eliot
Died Dec. 7, 1750. Aged 68.
On the South panel:
In Memoriam.
Lt. Col. WILLIAM VAUGHAN
Son of Lt. Gov. George and Elizabeth Vaughan
Born Sept. 12, 1703
Graduated at Harvard Coll. 1722
Projected the Expedition against
Louisburg 1745, and successfully led the
Assaulting Column
Died in London Dec. 1746.
Engraved upon the North panel is the simple legend:
VAUGHAN.

Those who are fascinated with the ghost stories associated with the Vaughn tomb have told of strange photographs taken at the gravesite. Visitors have photos of orbs around the tomb, thought to be spirits or light anomalies. There is a streetlight close to the burial ground, but even photos taken from odd angles have captured unusual images that cannot be explained.

When I visited the gravesite on one occasion, there was an unusual occurrence that was witnessed by several people who accompanied me. One night as the light from my flashlight illuminated the gravestone, a stream of water began to pour from a seam in the stone, as if an invisible faucet had been turned on. The day had been dry with no rain whatsoever. The stream of water poured out of the space in the stone for a few minutes, but the rest of the tombstone remained dry and undisturbed. Photographs taken of the strange occurrence revealed a number of orbs around the tomb. In the opposite corner of the burial ground is an area that stirs strong emotions in some visitors. One tall, slanting tombstone lists the sad death of two children, both under the age of three, who died during the yellow fever epidemic in Portsmouth during the late eighteenth century. A ship named *Mentor* came back from Martinique carrying coffee, molasses, and the dreaded yellow fever. The ship belonged to Thomas Sheafe, a local merchant. The epidemic killed nearly one hundred people and struck a few families especially hard, sometimes claiming all of their children's lives. In his local book called *Brewster's Rambles about Portsmouth*, Brewster described what happened during the dark times of the yellow fever:

> People were hurried to their graves hastily. No procession attended. Soon as the breath left the body, and perhaps sometimes before, it was immediately put in a tarred sheet and rough box; slid from a chamber window to a cart. Like the burial of Sir John Moore, they were hurried off at dead of night, by the lantern dimly burning.

Many visitors to this grave feel a deep sense of grief when approaching it. The stone has the words "Two Infant Children" carved in large letters, and visitors sometimes tearfully back away from the stone. Other people have felt an unseen presence in front of the gravestone, and have dowsed with pendulums to determine if spirits are present. The pendulums would swing wildly in this location, indicating that a spirit or spirits are close to the gravesite. Perhaps the parents of the infants are kneeling in sadness for the loss of their children. What else could explain the powerful feeling of grief that descends upon visitors to the grave?

One particular ghost story is a local favorite concerning Elizabeth Pierce, who was buried in the cemetery in 1717. Elizabeth's gravestone is a remarkably well-preserved example from the Colonial period. The carvings on it depict a winged skull and hourglass in which all of the sand has run out (symbolizing that time is fleeting). She is thought to have passed away from consumption (known today as tuberculosis) at the age of forty-two, and she has no visible relations buried near her. Visitors to Elizabeth's grave describe being gently "pushed" back as they are walking away from her stone. On one occasion a little girl about six years old was visiting the burial ground, and while inspecting the stone very closely, said to her mother, "You know, she's very lonely and sad." Her mother believed her daughter was somehow connecting with the spirit of Elizabeth. It seems that children are drawn to the Elizabeth's story and they love to look at the details on her stone, hoping to sense the touch of Elizabeth's ghost as they walk away.

A local newspaper reporter along with a group of about fifteen people noticed a most unusual formation taking shape in the sky while they were visiting Elizabeth's grave. On what had been a dark and cloudy day, the sky above the graveyard appeared to change. A few small pink wisps of clouds that looked just like angels suddenly appeared. While these shapes hovered in the sky for only a few moments, the witnesses say it was easy to discern heads and wings, not unlike the images seen carved on the gravestones. These pink cloud formations stood out against the blackened sky and were quite striking, especially after just discussing Elizabeth's story by her grave.

The Point of Graves is a burial ground that deserves the greatest respect, not just for its sheer history, but also for the stories and stones that exist there in an ancient setting where ghosts still roam among the living.

SOUTH CEMETERY, PORTSMOUTH, NH

Then a young lover came beside its dwelling,
To a maiden his gentle love-tale telling;
He pluck'd a rose from out of the shade—
'Twas not bright as the cheek on which it was laid:
The tale was told in the sunny noon,
Yet the same was heard by the rising moon.

—L.E. Landon, 1835, The Spirit and The Angel of Death

On the corner of Sagamore Avenue and South Street is a group of burial grounds collectively known as the South Cemetery, one of the oldest in Portsmouth. The first interments in the cemetery are believed to have taken place during seventeenth century; however, there are no records that indicate the details of these early burials. Auburn Cemetery, Proprietor's Burial Ground, Sagamore Cemetery and Harmony Grove are all combined at the South Cemetery.

The grounds are popular for recreational walks with pleasing shady lanes accented by tall trees. Part of the cemetery overlooks an inlet of the Piscataqua River. In the fall, the foliage in the cemetery turns blazing colors of gold, red and orange, presenting a colorful carpet of leaves across the grounds. There is a wide variety of gravestones and markers throughout the area including eighteenth-century winged skulls, an Egyptian-styled sarcophagus and several mausoleums. There are literally hundreds of examples of Victorian funerary images on the gravestones from the nineteenth century.

Several notable people are buried in the South Cemetery, including Revolutionary War soldiers, ship captains and a Supreme

Court Justice. Antethe Matea and Karen Anne Christensen were buried here in 1873; both were victims of the infamous ax murders on Smuttynose island, just off the coast. Their terrifying story inspired the book and movie *The Weight of Water*. The grave marker of Portsmouth's robber baron, Frank Jones, is the tallest in the cemetery (and in the state of New Hampshire) reaching 28 feet in height.

It is hard to imagine that this peaceful area once served as one of the hanging grounds for Portsmouth during the eighteenth century. The execution of Ruth Blay is one of the most curious of tales to come out of those years. In 1768, Ruth Blay was a pregnant twenty-five-year-old unmarried schoolteacher from Hampton, New Hampshire. She delivered the stillborn child herself, and was so distraught and frightened that she buried the baby beneath the floorboards of the school. One of Ruth's students witnessed the incident, believing Ruth had murdered her baby, ran home to tell her parents. Ruth was indicted for concealing the death of an illegitimate child, despite the fact that there was no surety as to whether her child was stillborn or murdered. She was quickly found guilty and sentenced to death by hanging. Although several reprieves were issued to halt the execution, she was finally sentenced to hang on December 31, 1768, in what is now the South Cemetery.

Sheriff Packer presided over Ruth's hanging and he had received word that a final governor's reprieve was being issued. The documentation was slow to arrive to the hand of the sheriff and he had planned to have his dinner on time that day—precisely at noon. The sheriff refused to wait any longer for the pardon to arrive and he insisted that the hanging take place at the designated hour. Ruth was brought by cart through the streets of downtown Portsmouth and her screams were described as heart wrenching as she pleaded her innocence. A crowd had assembled to witness Ruth's agonizing end and they implored Sheriff Packer to wait for the pardon to arrive. Sheriff Packer had become annoyed by the crowd and precisely at the stroke of noon the Sheriff quickly ordered the cart drawn away. Ruth's hanging body twisted in the frosty December air, as the crowd around her stood and stared in disbelief.

As Ruth's lifeless body cast it's shadow on the ground, the clattering sound of a horse and rider broke the silence. A messenger carrying the pardon from the Governor rode up and placed the paperwork in the hand of Sheriff Packer.

Disgusted by the actions of Sheriff Packer the townspeople assembled later that day and marched over to the sheriff's house. The angry mob burned an effigy of him on the lawn. But despite the outcry and anger of the people, Packer remained sheriff for a few more years and died quite wealthy. Ruth Blay was quietly buried in an unmarked grave near the pond at the cemetery. It was a few years after Ruth's death that the state of New Hampshire did away with the death penalty, and it's ironic to think that the last person executed was an innocent woman.

The tale was memorialized in the "Ballad of Ruth Blay," published in Thomas Bailey Aldrich's *An Old Town By The Sea*. The following is an excerpt:

BALLAD OF RUTH BLAY
by Albert Laighton (1859)

"When at last, in tones of warning,
From its high and airy tower,
Slowly with its tongue of iron,
Tolled the bell the fatal hour;
Like the sound of distant billows,
When the storm is wild and loud,
Breaking on the rocky headland,
Ran a murmur through the crowd.
And a voice among them shouted,
'Pause before the deed is done;
We have asked reprieve and pardon
For the poor misguided one.'
But these words of Sheriff Packer
Rang above the swelling noise:
'Must I wait and lose my dinner?
Draw away the cart, my boys!'

Nearer came the sound and louder,
Till a steed with panting breath,
From its sides the white foam dripping,
Halted at the scene of death;

And a messenger alighted,
Crying to the crowd, 'Make way!
This I bear to Sheriff Packer;
'Tis a pardon for Ruth Blay!"

Rumored to be one of the most haunted locations in Portsmouth, the South cemetery has a variety of ghostly tales. Seacoast resident Lothar Patten became a local celebrity when a documentary was filmed about him and his experiences with spirits. In this documentary, Lothar talked about the time he spent in Portsmouth's cemeteries. He believed that he not only could sense the spirits, but that he could see them, and described a spirit in the South Cemetery named Debra. He said that he saw a warm, inviting bright light approach him from across the grounds when she made herself known to him. According to Lothar she was a gentle spirit who was lonely and would communicate with him. He believed he had found a friend and a felt kinship with this lost soul. He even said that on a few occasions she appeared to him outside of the cemetery. Lothar passed away in 2008 and some people believe that now his spirit is peacefully on the other side with Debra.

The cemetery is most intriguing around sunset, when many believe the spirits are the most active. One resident, while walking through the cemetery, claims to have felt a strong presence with her. She became frightened and ran to her car to drive home, but even at home still felt the presence. She was so disturbed, that she called a psychic to come help her dispel the ghost.

Visitors have said that during the sunset hours they have felt something or someone pulling at their clothes. Those who are curious about the spirits will bring cameras to the grounds at night to conduct what is known as spiritography, the study of ghostly images on film. Spiritography is the belief that photographs are a type of communication between the spirit world and the current consciousness, or plane, in which we exist. Spirit photography is one of the earliest types of photography and has been around since 1839.. Many people believe they have captured images of apparitions at the South Cemetery. It has been suggested that one of the best areas for taking pictures is in the older sections nearest the South Street Entrance.

One of the other legends about the South Cemetery relates to two glowing gravestones in the vicinity of the pond in the graveyard. There is no logical explanation as to why these two stones glow eerily late at night. While there are several other stones in the same area none of those appear to glow. The streetlights are said to be at such an angle that they do not reflect off of these glowing stones. To view this phenomenon stand on the highest part of the hill looking towards the pond, in the graveyard late at night and you'll see this unusual phenomenon. Some claims even mention the appearance of a dark figure standing behind these glowing stones.

With all of the experiences people have relayed about the South cemetery it is easy to believe that there are some spirits who may not be at rest, but wander the grounds in the shadows of the gravestones.

Meeting House Burial Ground, Henniker, New Hampshire

When I die prepare my welcome grave
Where the eternal ocean rolls his wave
Rough though the blast;
Still let his free born breeze
Which freshness wafts to earth from endless seas
Sigh o'er my sleep.

—*Mrs. John Hunter, 1793*, a Scottish Poet

Apopular ghost story comes out of Henniker, New Hampshire, and has all the fascination of pirates, a haunted house and a haunted grave.

Mary Wilson Wallace was born at sea aboard the ship the *Wolf*, just outside of Boston harbor on July 28, 1720. The ship that carried Scotch-Irish immigrants to New England was captured by the pirate Don Pedro. Don Pedro was known for being ruthless and he could have killed everyone on the ship and taken it for himself, but when he learned that there was a newborn child on board that changed him. He asked Elizabeth Fulton-Wilson if she would name her new born daughter Mary after his beloved mother, and if she did he would let the ship go. Mrs. Wilson readily agreed and Don Pedro left the ship returning one final time carrying gifts. One of the gifts he brought was a bolt of beautiful green Chinese silk and he asked that when Mary was old enough a wedding gown be made for her out of the fabric.

After arriving in Boston, Mr. Wilson died and his widow and daughter continued to Londonderry, New Hampshire. Mrs. Wilson settled into Londonderry and eventually remarried. For many years the town held a celebration to remember the deliverance of the people on the ship that had been held captive, including Mary. Mary was described as being very tall, with long red flowing hair, a wonderful personality, and elegant manners. She spoke with a distinct brogue.

In December of 1742 Ocean Born Mary (as she had come to be known) married a Scottish immigrant James Wallace. Mary's wedding gown was made out of the Chinese silk that Don Pedro had given to her mother. Today a piece of her wedding dress is in the Henniker Town Library. Ocean Born Mary died on February 13, 1814 and is buried in the cemetery behind Henniker's original Town Hall.

Mary Wilson Wallace's grave is easy to find and bears a willow and urn as well as a small plaque at the base which reads, "Ocean Born Mary." This quiet cemetery on the edge of a hill offers beautiful foliage in the fall and the large stone wall that borders the front of the grounds adds a distinctly New England character. The giant pine trees that stand as sentinels at the entrance gates to the cemetery, have thick roots extending throughout the grounds. A small white building near the corner of the cemetery was built in 1842, to store the town hearse. The marble gravestones throughout the cemetery are streaked with gray giving them a rather ominous appearance.

Many stories of a ghostly presence have been recounted, and it is believed that Mary is the source. Two police officers in the late 1960s saw a spirit rise from Mary's grave, climb aboard a phantom carriage, and ride across town. Other people claim to have felt the presence of a spirit while standing at her grave. Curious visitors attempting to make contact with her spirit through electronic devices describe recording whispers and knocking sounds at her grave, and they maintain that there was no logical explanation for the noise.

Auguste Roy of Wisconsin purchased the house that Mary lived in during her time in Henniker and he opened it up for tours. He told visitors of a rocking chair by the fireplace that rocked on its own, and said there was a sensation of someone standing next to the hearth. He claimed to have seen Mary at the top of the staircase in the house. The house was even investigated by Dr. Hans Holzer, a paranormal expert, who agreed that the house was haunted.

Ocean Born Mary's life was fascinating, but equally compelling are the various tales of her afterlife. Should you decide to visit her grave maybe you'll hear the whispers.

RHODE ISLAND

HISTORICAL CEMETERY NUMBER 22, EXETER

When the sun in the west is sinking,
Its last crimson gleam I see,
I dream in the evening twilight,
Beloved one of thee.
When my soul with care is burdened,
And weary my heart may be,
Thy love like a rainbow of promise,
Will gild die future for me.
And I list for the southern breezes
To waft a sweet message from dice;
As a priceless gem, thy devotion,
Enshrined in my heart will be.

—*Cordelia Elizabeth Moore, "I will remember Thee"*

The legendary story of Mercy Brown is probably one of Rhode Island's most intriguing tales. The secret lies buried in Historical Cemetery Number 22, behind Exeter's Chestnut Hill Baptist Church on Route 102, on a hill framed by rustling dark woods. George Brown and his wife, Mary, along with their five children, lived on a small family farm in rural Exeter, Rhode Island. The family's tragic ordeal began on December 8, 1883, when George's wife succumbed to consumption (a.k.a. tuberculosis) at the age of thirty-six. Less than six months later, George's eldest daughter, Mary Olive, age twenty, also passed away from consumption on June 6, 1884.

Seven years later, George's only son, Edwin, contracted the disease. In hopes that he would find a cure during the mineral water craze of the nineteenth century, Edwin left Rhode Island

and headed west for Colorado Springs. It wasn't long after Edwin left that his sister, Mercy Lena, became ill. The disease had quickly progressed, and at the age of nineteen, on January 18, 1892, Mercy died. Since it was winter, the ground was frozen, and Mercy could not be buried right away, so her body was placed inside a crypt near the rest of her family. Mercy was eventually interred in the family plot located in the Chestnut Hill Cemetery in Exeter.

Edwin returned to Rhode Island and his health worsened after Mercy's funeral. George Brown became more worried and grew anxious as the days passed. George could not accept the possibility of losing his only son and two surviving daughters. He needed to find a way to put an end to his misery. George's neighbors were quite frightened of the situation as well, and the answer to his personal plague seemed to be entwined with folklore.

Superstitious townsfolk suggested to George that perhaps one of his deceased family members was rising from the grave to devour Edwin's life. George and Edwin Brown decided that it was not consumption that was afflicting him, rather he was being attacked by a vampire. It was uncertain if the vampire was Mercy Brown, or Mercy's mother or sister. The decision was made to exhume the corpses in the cemetery. With the assistance from Doctor Metcalf (from nearby Wickford), the bodies of the three women were exhumed. The bodies of George's wife and daughter, Mary, appeared to be in an advanced state of decay, as they had both been deceased for approximately ten years. However, when the body of Mary was examined, they found that her body was still fresh, and it seemed to have shifted in the coffin. Further, when the doctor cut Mercy's heart out, he discovered that there was still blood in it. The heart was placed on a stone in the cemetery and burned. The ashes were mixed with medicine and given as a cure to Edwin Brown to ingest.

Despite the belief that this practice would save Edwin, he died two months later on May 9, 1892. It was soon discovered that consumption was actually spread by bacteria. Embalming corpses was also becoming more common, further dispelling the vampire superstition.

The fascination with Mercy Brown's story transcended the strange events after her death. In 1897, when Bram Stoker, author of *Dracula*, died, newspaper accounts of Mercy Brown's exhumation were found in his personal files. Local literary horror author, H.P. Lovecraft mentioned Mercy's tale in his short story, *The Shunned House.*

George Brown died in 1922 at the age of eighty and he is also buried in the cemetery. The crypt where Mercy's body was examined is a short walk from the Brown family plot, and there is a debate as to which rock Mercy's heart was burned on. Mercy has the most visited grave in the cemetery, and people often leave mementos on her gravestone. Many of the locals believe that Mercy's ghost wanders the cemetery grounds and can be seen most often in October under the moonlight. Other people believe that if you knock on Mercy's gravestone three times, she will appear or speak to you.

Great Swamp Burial Ground, South Kingstown Area

THE GRAVE OF NINIGRET.
A stricken pine — a weed-grown mound
On the upland's rugged crest,
Point where the hunted Indian found
At length a place of rest.
Thou withered tree, by lightning riven.
Of bark and leaf bereft,
With lifeless arms erect to heaven,
Of thee a remnant's left ;
The bolt that broke thy giant pride
Yet spared the sapling green ;
And tall and stately by thy side
'Twill show what thou hast been.
But of the Narragansett race
Nor kith, nor blood remains ;
Save that perchance a tainted trace
May lurk in servile veins.
The mother's shriek, the warrior's yell
That rent the midnight air
When Christians made yon swamp a hell,
No longer echo there.
The cedar brake is yet alive —
But not with human tread —
Within its shade the plover thrive,
The otter makes its bed.
The red fox hath his hiding-place
Where ancient foxes ran.
How keener than the sportsman's chase
The hunt of man by man!

—Henry Mann, 1896

° 91 °

A severely weatherworn sign stands at the entrance to the Great Swamp in South Kingstown, Rhode Island, where the Great Swamp Fight against the Narragansett Tribe occurred in 1675. The marker reads, "Three-quarters of a mile to the southward on an island in the Great Swamp the Narragansett Indians were decisively defeated by the united forces of the Massachusetts Bay, Connecticut, and Plymouth colonies, Sunday, December 19, 1675." Many of the early chapters in New England's history have their own elements of unimaginable dread, yet some of them remain largely forgotten. As grave markers sink slowly into the ground with the passage of time, the stories get older and seem more remote to us.

The Narragansett were a powerful tribe of Indians, and in 1675 they allied themselves with King Philip, the infamous Wampanoag Sachem. The Narragansett tribe supported the Wampanoag Tribe's efforts to regain land in Massachusetts in the conflict known as King Philips War. During the frigid hours of December 19 (in what is now Charlestown, Rhode Island), a military force of one thousand men, including Puritans from Plymouth Colony and Connecticut, planned an attack on a group of mostly women, children, and elderly men living at an Indian winter camp in the Great Swamp.

The attack came swiftly and was very fierce, with the Indians soon losing their advantage. Hundreds of wigwams and their stockpiles of winter supplies were burned as the Narragansett Indian's fort was destroyed. It is believed that upwards of six hundred Indians were killed or captured, and some who escaped were hunted down and killed. Many of those captured were sold into slavery in Bermuda or the Caribbean. This battle is considered the beginning of the end for the strength and unity of the Narragansett, whose original territory covered most of Rhode Island.

According to the manuscript of the Rev. W. Ruggles, he described the incident as follows:

The shrieks and cries of the women and children, the yelling of the warriors, exhibited a most horrible and appalling scene, so that it greatly moved some of the soldiers. They were in much doubt and they afterwards seriously inquired whether burning their enemies alive could be consistent with humanity and the benevolent principle of the gospel.

A decaying monument stands in the old Indian burial ground near the swamp. Sinking in the ground underfoot is a handful of humble fieldstone markers, indicating just a few of what are said to be upwards of eighty graves of the Narragansett Indians. Some years ago, when homes were being built in the area of the burial ground, bones of the Indians were dug up revealing that they were buried in the fetal position with their head pointed towards the sun, which was tradition for the tribe. Because of the excavations, it is believed that the remains are close to the surface. Today, descendents of the Narragansett tribe still visit the site to look for any signs of vandalism and to perform ancient rites at the burial ground.

The nearby swamp has been a state-managed wildlife area since 1950. The large amount of waterfowl and beautiful birds attract people to the area, especially during the bird's migratory months. Many people take pleasure in kayaking through the variety of waterways around the swamp.

Ghostly stories have come from those who have visited the unassuming burial ground. With all of the wildlife surrounding the area, it is said that the woods will often fall suddenly quiet with a peculiar silence. A palpable somber and sad mood has been experienced by those who tread these grounds as well. Piercing screams have been heard echoing from the swamp, along with the sounds of gunfire and uncontrollable sobbing. Sensations of being watched and wintry breezes have sent many visitors running back to their vehicles. No matter if it's the ghosts or just the memory of the terror that unfolded here in 1675, this little burial ground has a spirit and presence that is undeniable.

MAINE

Eastern Cemetery, Portland

Within a city's throbbing heart,
Where life is bright and gay,
There nestles, from the world apart,
A graveyard old and gray.
O'er mossy walls the ivy falls, But now the evening shadow creeps
In slender sprays of green. Across the harbor bar,
And silently the lichen crawls And o'er the tranquil azure deeps
The narrow mounds between. Climbs up a lonely star.
Here oft, in childhood's early hours, O angel Night! thy dewy wing
My footsteps fondly strayed, Enfolds the spirit's dream,
From pleasure's warm, sunshiny And to the fevered heart you bring
Into the realms of shade, bowers, A balm from Kedron's stream.
And pensively my fancy roamed The subtle web that fancy weaves
Adown the years to be, Lies broken on the tomb,
Where fairy castles, jewel-domed, While in the path of rustling leaves
Gleamed through the mists for me. I wander through the gloom.

—Millie Concord, "Among The Shadows"

The gloom of one of the oldest cemeteries in Maine doesn't seem to be terribly evident during the day. The modern city of Portland has sprung up around the Eastern Cemetery. This ancient burial ground was chartered in 1668 at the base of Munjoy Hill and has many stories to share. A great number of the early settlers were buried here including those who were victims of brutal Indian attacks. Twelve men that were killed at the historic September 21, 1689, massacre are buried here. Just a few years after the 1689 massacre, thirteen men were killed by a party of Indians in an ambush near the burial ground and their remains were deposited into the Eastern Cemetery.

Initially burials only took place in the southeastern section of the cemetery, where there are numerous unmarked graves. Until 1820 the rest of the cemetery was used as a public common. Tales of unrest, in addition to ghosts, seem to plague this final resting place. George Cleeve, who is given credit as the father of Portland, designated this land to be a burial ground. As one of the first settlers of the city, his home was built in the area of the burial ground, and upon his passing in 1666, his was one of the first burials to take place in the cemetery. However, two hundred years later, just after Portland's devastating Great Fire of 1866, Cleeve's silent slumber was disturbed.

During the rebuilding, a retaining wall was built along Federal Street, and in doing so, part of the hillside of the burial ground was excavated. This burrowing into the hillside section of the cemetery disturbed a number of the early settler's remains, including George Cleeve. All of the soil that was dug up—along with everything that was in it—was removed and brought over to Back Cove and deposited as fill. For a burial ground that has such strong ties to this very old settlement and its history, it is a shame to learn of the disregard that was shown to these graves. Today, the Back Cove boasts one of the oldest and most popular recreational trails in Portland. It is a curious thought that those who enjoy visiting the trails do not realize that they are passing by the founding fathers of the city as their remains lie scattered at the bottom of the cove. Perhaps one day when the tide goes out and the cove turns to mud flats, the bones from the old burial ground will reappear as a grim reminder of what occurred in 1866.

Just adjacent to the burial ground, during the eighteenth century, were the stocks and the whipping post. During the American Revolution, many soldiers were whipped for misdemeanors at the whipping post. At the eastern edge of the burial ground was the town pound, which confined stray animals until they were claimed. Comprised of about seven acres, the graveyard once featured an enormous Norway pine tree that was visible from Portland Harbor.

However the tree was blown down during a howling storm in 1815. The Eastern Cemetery was the only public burial place in the city until 1829. Within the cemetery are believed to be approximately seventy-five underground tombs. The largest and oldest is that of Joseph H. Ingraham, and is rumored to contain over sixty bodies.

In the southwest corner of the grounds is an area of unmarked graves that was used as an area for Quaker burials. Two other unmarked sections of the graveyard served as an African American burial ground, and an area for "strangers" that was set aside for the poor and unknown. In a peculiar tradition, the city of Portland allowed for the burial of two bodies per grave in the "strangers" area.

In the 1863 book, *The Charter and Ordinances of the City of Portland* by John T. Fagan, he described some of the regulations and fees associated with the burial ground:

SECTION 34. The undertakers shall be allowed to charge and receive the following fees for their services, to wit: For opening church and carrying the body into the same for funeral services, an additional fee of two dollars. For services attending funeral and depositing the body of an adult in the city tomb, four dollars; for removing and interring the same in Eastern Cemetery, one dollar and fifty cents. For attending funeral services and depositing the body of a child in the city tomb, three dollars; for removing and interring the same in Eastern Cemetery, one dollar.

Some of Portland's infamous are buried here, including two men, Thomas Bird and Solomon Goodwin, who were hung for murder in the late eighteenth century. The cemetery also contains the grave of Daniel Manly who holds the distinction of being Portland's first bank robber in 1818. It is easy to find the city's maritime heritage in the cemetery, as there are so many epitaphs that tell of those who met their fate on the seas. The ranks of captains and crew all mingle their dust in this ancient bone yard. These stones offer interesting epitaphs some of which read "Lost at Sea," "Executed for murder on the high seas," and "Killed by a fall from masthead." Further readings tell the departed's stories in more detail:

In memory of Mrs. Mary Stonehouse of Boston relict of the late Capt. Robert Stonehouse, she was drowned from the Portland Packet. July 12 1807. Aged 62 years. From the cold bosom of the wave, Where others found a watr'y grave, This lifeless corpse was borne, and here The friends of virtue drop the tear That mourn the much lamented dead, But oh! What bitter tears are shed For fathers, mothers, babes who sleep In the dark mansions of the deep. Then young & old, rich & poor prepare For God may summons when you're not aware.

In memory of
LIEUT. WILLIAM R. LLOYD,
of the British Navy,
who died March 24, 1819:
aged 23 years.
A native of
Plymouth in England.
He came to this Country for his health:
but it was the will of providence, that
he should here finish his mortal career.

By strangers honour'd & by strangers mourn'd.

One of the tallest monuments in the burial ground is that of the memorial to Colonel William Tyng. It stands at ten feet high and is made of red freestone and marble. This memorial authorized by his wife remembers the Colonel as a man who received his commission from British General Gage in Boston. Then, in 1774, he fled to New York, and then Nova Scotia, but returned to Maine in 1793 and settled in nearby Gorham, where he passed away in 1807.

As part of the tragic seafaring history stands the grave of Captain Jacob Adams and his wife. He was Captain of the ill-fated schooner named *Charles* that carried a young Lydia Carver and her bridal party back from Boston, Massachusetts, in 1807. The schooner sank in a storm on Richmond Island on Cape Elizabeth. There were no survivors.

Two famous heroes from one of the most important naval engagements of the war of 1812 are buried in the Eastern Cemetery. There are a variety of accounts about this infamous battle between the *Boxer* and the *Enterprise,* which occurred off the coast of Pemaquid, Maine. On Monday September 6, 1813, the United States brigantine *Enterprise* arrived in Portland Harbor, bringing her prize, his Majesty's ship, the *Boxer,* captured the previous day after a well-fought battle that lasted just forty-five minutes. Both commanders, Capt. William Burrows of the *Enterprise* and Capt. Samuel Blyth of the Boxer, were mortally wounded in the engagement. The brave commander of the *Enterprise* remained on deck where he lay, insisting that he not be carried below. When the battle was won and the sword of the enemy was presented to him, the dying hero clasped his hands and said, "I am satisfied. I die contented." That night he departed this world and the Boxer surrendered the next afternoon. The *Enterprise* brought into Portland sixty-four prisoners. She had lost but two men, and twelve were wounded.

The two captains, each not yet thirty years old, were prepared for burial with crowds of people assembling from far and wide, on foot, on horseback, and even some by an ox team. Their graves were memorialized in the 1855 poem by Henry Wadsworth Longfellow,

My Lost Youth

I remember the sea-fight far away,
How it thundered o'er the tide!
And the dead captains, as they lay
In their graves o'erlooking the tranquil bay
Where they in battle died.

Ghostly tales are told of the two fearless captains. The apparitions of each are said to appear by their gravesides after midnight engaged in a war of words. This shouting match has been witnessed by those curious enough to peek in through the locked gates of the cemetery. The spirits are said to have an awareness of whoever might be watching, and as soon as they turn to look towards the gates, the phantoms disappear behind their dignified grave markers, leaving nothing behind, except for a mysterious fine mist lingering in the air.

Upon a visit to the cemetery, one would find a variety of young trees that have been recently planted to replace the multitudes of trees that have been cut down over the years, leaving the burial ground very sparse. Near the Congress Street entrance is a very attractive Gothic Revival cottage, underneath which was the city tomb that was used during the winter months. In 1868, it was reported that there were 111 bodies awaiting burial in the spring, when the ground thawed. Today this building is used as a storage shed for the cemetery. Along the same entrance there is a beautiful black iron fence and gate, which were actually salvaged several years ago from renovations at the Portland High School. This intricate fence adds to the Gothic charm of the entrance to the burial ground, and invites one to peer between the railings to catch a glimpse of the past.

There are numerous plaques within and just outside of the cemetery. One plaque declares the burial ground as a National Historic Site in January of 1974. It further reads, "Here lie the hardy courageous early settlers, the men and women who founded and defended this area, who made history in civil life, government, law, the arts, education, religion, in the state and in the nation." Another plaque that stands just outside of the cemetery gates informs visitors that the graveyard is the final resting place for many of those Portland residents who were abolitionists. These people provided safe houses as part of the Underground Railroad, campaigned against slavery, and assisted African Americans to freedom. This spot on the Portland Freedom Trail remembers those who made a difference during these times.

Tragic circumstances affected this cemetery from July 1988 to August 1989 when 1,943 gravestones were vandalized and destroyed in cemeteries across Portland. Most of those stones dated from the first 150 years of Portland's burials. Today there are no stones that remain from the seventeenth century, and the oldest remaining stone dates from May 23, 1717.

This cemetery was so full in the late nineteenth century that bodies were packed into the ground in odd angles and dispositions. Today the cemetery is getting assistance from a group appropriately named Spirits Alive, which was formed in 2006 to help preserve one of the most fascinating cemeteries in Maine. Their efforts are to protect and preserve this very spirited burial ground.

THE MASS GRAVE IN THE EASTERN PROMENADE, PORTLAND

✤✤✤

An almost-forgotten burial ground in the eastern promenade section of Portland is located at the foot of Quebec Street. A boulder marks a mass grave for twenty-one prisoners of war from the War of 1812. The British Warship *Regulus* was sailing from Quebec to Boston with American soldiers that were taken prisoner at the battle of Queenstown. The ship arrived in Portland under a flag of truce and anchored in the harbor. Lt. Colonel Winfield Scott (also known as "Old Fuss and Feathers") was the commander of the ship. When the ship arrived, there were twenty-four very ill men who were hospitalized in town. Ailing from malnutrition, fever, and dysentery, twenty-one of them died within a month. A bronze plaque attached to the boulder lists the names of the unfortunate souls who never made it home.

OLD COMMON CEMETERY, HARPSWELL

O! Bury me not in the sunless tomb,
When Death in its chain has bound me;
Let me not sleep where the shadows loom, In the stifled air around me;
Where the bones of the scarce-remembered dead
Keep a ghastly watch round my coffin bed!
O, bury me not 'mid the ceaseless hum Of the city's wild commotion,
Where the steps of a thoughtless crowd might come,
Like the waves of a troubled ocean.
In the eye of love should a tear-drop start,
'Twould crush it back on the swollen heart!
But bury me out in the wild, wild wood,
Where the sunlit leaves are dancing,
Where the rills leap out with a merry shout,
And the brooks in the light are glancing ;
Let my bed be made by the fond and true,
Who can bear to weep when I'm shut from view.
In the forest home — in the wild wood home —
With the arching limbs above me,
Where the sunbeams creep for a quiet sleep,
To my grave, like dear friends that love me,
Let me rest 'mid the bloom of the pure and fair ;
I should know that the blossoms I loved were there.

—*Harriet Marion Stephens*, "My Grave"

The town of Harpswell, Maine, incorporated in 1731, is on a dramatic peninsula that reaches into Casco Bay and

---

* Author of many poems and stories, she passed away at the age of thirty-five in East Hampden, Maine.

incorporates forty-seven offshore islands with over 216 miles of coastline. Local lore suggests the islands are haunted. Some claim visits there improve their health, and there is believed to be buried treasure protected by ghosts on some of the islands.

The Old Common Cemetery in Harpswell is a picturesque, classic New England cemetery. At the front of the burial ground is the beautiful, old First Parish Meetinghouse, which is a registered historic landmark, constructed between 1757 and 1759. Amazingly the meetinghouse is so valued by the National Association of Architects that twelve blueprints were filed with the National Archives in Washington, DC, so that the building could be recreated if it was ever destroyed. The dramatic interior of the meetinghouse features a ten-foot-high pulpit and sounding board as well as pumpkin pine pews. The graveyard is surrounded by a broad stone wall. The back of the burial ground is thick with young trees that add to the beauty of the grounds. Thousands of delicate lily of the valley flowers bloom at the entrance and along the edges of the cemetery in the spring. Lily of the valley has been used as a symbol of the resurrection throughout time, especially on gravestone art.

In 2001, the town did a major renovation and restoration to the graveyard, clearing away brush and overgrown grasses. As part of the refurbishment, the town straightened and cleaned many of the gravestones, making some readable once again. The oldest readable stone was placed in the burial ground sometime around 1758, while earlier wooden markers have been lost to time and the elements. The quality and variety of the carvings and some very lyrical epitaphs create a reflective atmosphere in this welcoming place. The cemetery was in use until about 1900, when it became necessary to refuse further interments because old graves were being uncovered whenever a new grave was dug.

There are many stones that record the names of the early settlers throughout the grounds. The variety of epitaphs will keep the curious reading throughout their visit to the burial ground.

In Memory Of
Miss Elizabeth Eaton
Who exchanged worlds
January 13, 1806, Age 65
Those active limbs in this cold grave are laid,
Which I possest & to have nature paid,
That debt you owe & soon you must repay
Prepare for death & the great rising day

There is a wonderful collection of eighteenth-century and nineteenth-century funerary art, including a young angel riding on clouds, pointing skyward to the heavens and a hand reaching through the clouds plucking a tender rosebud from a bush. An intricately carved cherub wears an elaborate headdress on one stone, and there are a variety of winged skulls, cherubs, setting suns, and funerary urns.

A particularly sad epitaph is for little Freeman Allen:

Freeman M. Allen
Son of Elisha & Jane
March 29, 1851
Aged 2 years, 6 months
Our infant baby, the smiling boy
It's father's hope, it's mother's joy
In three years resigned its breath
His sparking eyes are boxed in death.

A small marble marker marks the grave of Baby Oliver, who was born and died the same day, November 10, 1879.

Goodwife, Hannah Stover, is buried somewhere unknown in an unmarked grave in the burial ground. Stover was a Quaker and she caused a great deal of scandal amongst the non-Quaker congregation by refusing to be present at the services in the old, square church. There were rumors throughout the village of her having a wilder and darker character. Originally from neighboring

Freeport, many people in town scorned her for being a witch.

There were accusations of Hannah's witch wiles by some of the fishermen, who claimed that she had cursed everything from their cows to fishing nets and the sails on their boats. There was one woman who had claimed that Hannah had bewitched her husband, Elkniah, and he could not see her witchy ways.

When Hannah died, the men of Harpswell Neck refused to carry her coffin to the meetinghouse for a Christian burial. Believing her to be a good person, the fisherman's wives went against their husband's wishes and carried the coffin to the burial ground instead. Upon their arrival, on a dreary November morning, the wives ran into an angry mob, led by Ezra Johnston, and a commotion at the gates of the burial ground commenced. Wild accusations filled the air, insisting that Hannah was a witch and should not be buried in the burial ground. An argument between Parson Eaton, one of the wives, and an angry Ezra Johnston ensued. He relayed the following accusation:

> Last Sabbath night I was woken in my sleep to the British bark off the point, and dragged by the Devil's imps up and down the sides till I was bruised and aching in every bone of my body. And I might have been killed but that daylight drew on, and with my own ears I heard Goodwife Stover say: "Let him go; 'tis almost cock-crowing." I knew her voice as well as I know my own, and that but two days before she died.

Mercy Stover, Hannah's stepdaughter, and Goody Cole spoke up and reminded the townspeople of Hannah's kindness and the unwavering help she gave to many of them.

But Ezra was unmoved, and continued his tirade. "Ye may take the witch-wife back," he said, with a roughness that was partly genuine and partly assumed to help him overcome some secret, lingering weakness. "Let her lie in some of the black places in the woods where she would foregather with her master the Devil; but her wicked body shall never poison the ground where Christian folk are buried. No grave in consecrated ground for the likes of her."

The exchange continued on in the shadow of the meetinghouse, and with everyone taking a side and voicing their opinion, Parson Eaton could barely be heard.

Goody Cole and some of the other women recalled how Hannah would sit by the bedsides of sick women, whom no one would visit, and how she visited a woman who had a terrible ordeal after the birth of her child. These women broke from the crowd and ran up to the coffin, bowing down on their knees in prayer.

Even still there was no man of Harpswell that stepped forward to carry the coffin of Hannah Stover into the burial ground. In the end, the fisherman's wives who had carried it down the shadowed road were the only ones who made sure that Hannah received a proper burial. They carried Hannah's coffin to her final resting place in the burial ground behind the meetinghouse.

The final exchange that day between Johnston and Parson Eaton offered no peace between the two parties.

"Ye have buried a witch," Johnston muttered under his breath, as they left the sacred spot.

"We have made the grave of a saint," Parson responded solemnly.

Another burial ground of note in Harpswell is located on the farmland once owned by Henry Barnes on the eastern side of Middle Bay, near the shore. In 1861, fourteen skeletons were disinterred. There were no headstones and it was said to have been an Indian burying ground by the appearance of the skeletons and the ornaments found on or near them. A party of seven Penobscot Indians, who once stopped at the burial ground on their way to Portland, confirmed the Indian burying ground and stated that there was once an Indian village close by.

GRAY CEMETERY

When the summer breeze is sighing
Mournfully along;
Or when autumn leaves are falling,
Sadly breathes the song.
Oft in dreams I see thee lying
On the battle plain,
Lonely, wounded, even dying,
Calling, but in vain.
If amid the din of battle
Nobly you should fall,
Far away from those who love you,
None to hear you call,
Who would whisper words of comfort,
Who would soothe your pain?

—Angie C. Beebe, 1903

At a scenic cemetery on top of a windy hill in Gray, Maine, along "Avenue H," there is a most curious grave. Due to a strange mistake during the dark days of the Civil War, flags of both the North and South fly in front of the well-kept "Stranger" grave. The grave marker simply reads:

STRANGER
A Soldier of the late war
died 1862
Erected by the Ladies of Gray

A perplexing story about this Civil War soldier has persisted for years. The little town of Gray sent proportionally more sons to the Civil War than any other town in Maine. Within the Gray Village Cemetery there are buried more than 178 Union soldiers. The Stranger's story, scarred by tears of tragedy and triumph, began with the death of Lt. Charles H. Colley, the twenty-nine-year-old son of Amos and Sarah Colley of Gray. When the war began, Colley joined the Federal forces, and was placed in Company B of the 10th Maine Volunteers.

Gray, a town of about fifteen hundred people, had sent nearly two hundred of its native sons to battle. Charles Colley was mortally wounded at the Battlefield of Cedar Mountain, Virginia, and died at the Alexandria Hospital in Virginia. His body was sent home for burial. However, when the casket was opened, it revealed the body of an unknown soldier in a gray Confederate uniform. It seemed that the army had put his casket on the wrong train. Incapable of correcting the mistake, and believing that the young man's family would want him to have a proper burial, the soldier was laid to rest in the town cemetery. In theory, the townspeople of Gray could have sent the body of the Stranger away, but they did not.

About a week later a second coffin containing the remains of Lieutenant Charles Colley arrived, and he was buried in the Colley family plot, not far from the Stranger's. When the war ended, money was collected by the Woman's Relief Corps of the Grand Army and they were able to obtain a gravestone for the unknown Confederate soldier. For many years The Daughters of the Confederacy, a women's heritage association, sent a Confederate flag, also known as the Stars and Bars, to be placed on the grave. In fact there were many people who were moved by the story and sent flags as well. The identity of the Stranger remains a mystery to the townspeople to this day. There is a bit of irony in the fact that an unidentified Confederate soldier dressed in gray, has his final resting place in Gray, Maine.

PINELAND CEMETERY, NEW GLOUCESTER

Remember me when I am gone away,
Gone far away into the silent land:
When you can no more hold me by the hand,
Nor I half turn to go yet turning stay.
Remember me when no more day by day
You tell me of our future that you planned:
Only remember me; you understand
It will be late to counsel then or pray.
Yet if you should forget me for a while
And afterwards remember, do not grieve:
For if the darkness and corruption leave
A vestige of the thoughts that once I had,
Better by far you should forget and smile
Than that you should remember and be sad.

—Christina Rossetti, "Remember"

A memorial located at the front of the Pineland Cemetery in New Gloucester, Maine, reads:

Nov. 1912
The people living on Malaga Island
New Meadows River, Maine
were relocated.
The people buried on the island were
Moved to Pineland's cemetery

A sad story comes to life in this burial ground, which contains the bodies of those who were disinterred for a burial ground on

Malaga Island, and those died at the nearby school for the "feeble-minded." The memories of those buried here reveal a gruesome chapter in history, one that is reflected in the cold uniformity of the evenly spaced grave markers. There is not so much as an epitaph or an angel on these very simple stones, as if they weren't even worth memorializing, but theirs is a story worth telling.

Pineland was a state facility that opened in 1908 as the Maine School for Feeble-Minded and closed as the Pineland Center in 1996. Due to the horrific conditions and abusive treatment of residents, Pineland was placed in federal receivership in 1976 and finally closed in 1996. Institutions like Pineland "treated" people with developmental and other disabilities by segregating, hiding, and even sterilizing children and adults, without their consent and based solely on their disability. There were many who died at the facility and their bodies were never claimed, so they were buried in the Pineland cemetery. There are dozens of stones here marking the existence of forgotten souls. It is quite amazing to walk around the burial ground and find many who had died under the age of twenty. In the early years, the graves were simply marked by a cylinder of cement with a number on top. In the 1950s, proper burial markers were placed in the cemetery, listing names and ages, when research could find them.

A couple miles up the road, Pineland has been completely refurbished and there are no signs of what used to be a dreary facility for many. Today, Pineland is a five thousand-acre working farm, with a variety of businesses housed in the former buildings on the property. An array of recreational events takes place on the rural property. The memories of those who passed through the doors, willingly or unwillingly, reside just down the road now in a peaceful burial ground.

There are also seventeen graves in this burial ground that mark another depressing tale of forgotten Mainers. Malaga Island, just off the coast of Phippsburg, was a small community of hardworking people. Some of the jobs of the people on Malaga were fishing, lobstering, clamming, and carpentry. All of the wives would stay at home and take care of their children as the fathers worked. They built little shacks for houses and used skiffs to get around on the water. With complete autonomy from Maine towns, the island became known as "No Man's Land." It was such a hard way of life for some on the island that many sought support from the mainland.

Those who shunned the islanders called Malaga an "eyesore" and a "maroon society." In addition, the people of the Island were a mixed race of Irish, Scottish, Portuguese, and African Americans, and some of them were runaway slaves. Mixed race marriages were common on the island and not a popular notion on the mainland at that time. The *Casco Bay Breeze* and other newspapers nosed around in the 1890s and printed stories about a "degenerate colony," whose indiscretions included use of tobacco and of tea, adding to the negative opinions of the mainlanders. A schoolhouse was built on the island and the children of the island were taught to read and write. An article in *Harper's* Magazine from 1909 describes the people of the island:

> So the "queer folk" live alone—and it is said that isolation develops eccentricity. The ocean creeps to the doors of their huts, and the winter waves thunder in their ears—and there are those who say that the din of the sea beats curious ideas into the head.

None of the neighboring towns wanted to support Malaga with the funds or supplies that they needed, and Phippsburg actually denied aid to the island and gave the island up as a "ward of the state." On July 14, 1911, Governor Plaisted and his council visited Malaga. The Governor deemed the conditions on the island as deplorable and he recommended burning down the shacks. On August 5, 1911, the plan was to give the people on Malaga two weeks to get off the island, and the Governor declared that the "Malaganians must move."

People on Malaga Island were paid for their homes, which were swiftly destroyed upon their exit from the island. Even the burial ground on the island was uprooted, and eighteen bodies were reburied in five large caskets in the Pineland burial ground. All of the nine headstones reflect the year of 1912, the year that they were reinterred here. One stone marks the grave of five children, and another marks the grave of three children.

Strangely some of those who were evicted from the island ended up being committed to the School for the Feeble Minded. Some died within a few years of leaving the island. For many others it was difficult for them to ever fit in with the mainland communities, as they were considered undesirable by the townspeople.

This quiet burial ground is for those whose stories are compelling, and their lives short. It is a reminder of a time where people were thrown away from society. Those who do know and care to visit the burial ground find it a place of tremendous sadness, and many paranormal groups conduct investigations here to try to connect with these lost souls.

OLD YORK VILLAGE BURIAL GROUND, YORK

I stretch my arms to clasp — the air!
I look, to find thou art not there.
I speak thy name — thou dost not hear,
And yet I feel that thou art near.

—*Horace Parker Chandler, 1896*

In 1641, a tract of land near the mouth of York River on the southern coast of Maine, just three miles square, was incorporated by Sir Ferdinando Gorges as the town of Agamenticus. Soon referred to as Gorgeana, the town has the distinction of being the nation's first chartered city. In 1652, when Massachusetts extended her jurisdiction over the province under a new interpretation of the boundaries of her charter, the name of the city was changed to York, and that of the province to Yorkshire. The town grew quickly in the 1700s, relying largely on maritime trade, farming, and fishing. Things declined briefly in the early 1800s, but soon turned around as York was discovered to be a wonderful vacation destination for summer tourists. York has now become a year-round tourist destination attracting visitors from far and near.

One of the oldest burying grounds in Maine, the graveyard of Old York village is steeped in local legends and lore. The burial ground was established around 1670, and the early grave markers were said to be simple wooden plank markers and fieldstones. Today, there are about 150 surviving gravestones, with the oldest dating from 1705. A variety of winged skulls and death heads can be found throughout the burial ground. Interments ended here in the mid nineteenth century because of over-crowding. When you look at the grounds today, there appear to be many open areas without gravestones, where bodies are buried without markers.

A large stone marker near the road remembers the "hardy pioneers" who suffered through a disastrous Indian attack in the winter of 1692. This marks the spot in the burial ground where there is a mass grave for approximately forty people, including Shubael Dummer, the town's minister. Known as the Candlemas raid, an unexpected assault was made early in the morning by upwards of three hundred Abenaki Indians under the command of the French. At the end of the rampage, approximately eighty villagers were taken hostage and forced to walk back to Canada. About a hundred other York residents were dead. Many undefended homes had been burned to the ground, supplies and food destroyed, and animals slaughtered. Many villagers fled to Canada, several dying along the way. The result of this attack made many children who survived relentless Indian fighters, as they sought revenge for the cruelties and indignities inflicted upon their parents. Historians still debate the reasons behind the Candlemas Raid today.

The most visited grave in the burial ground is that of Mary Nasson, who was alleged to have been the York Village witch. Her grave is quite obvious, as it is the only grave that has a large stone slab lying between the headstone and the footstone. Mary was an herbalist in the eighteenth century, and those who visited her for healing were promptly cured, much to the surprise of some people in the village. There are even allegations that Mary performed an occasional exorcism. With all of the mysterious activity surrounding Mary's life, some people thought that she might be, in fact, practicing witchcraft; an easy presumption for those who may have been superstitious.

When Mary passed away at the young age of twenty-nine, her husband commissioned a beautiful portrait stone by the Lamson family of stone carvers in Boston, Massachusetts. The carving is quite beautiful and depicts a woman with two very piercing eyes. The epitaph reads:

Here rests quite free from Life's
Distressing Care
A loving wife
A tender Parent dear ;
Cut down in midst of days
As you may see,
But — stop — my grief;
I soon shall equal be,
When death shall stop my breath;
And end my Time ;
God grant my Dust
May mingle, then, with thine.
Sacred to the memory of Mrs.
Mary Nasson, wife of Mr. Samuel
Nasson, who departed this life
Augst. 28th. 1774,
Aetat 29.

Mary's husband, Samuel, is not buried in the cemetery. It is rumored that upon his passing, his family had him buried in a family plot in Sanford, Maine. Folks remarked that the place of the large stone on Mary's grave was put there to keep Mary from rising from the grave. It was said that if you touched the headstone and then touched the stone slab, you could feel that the slab on the ground was much warmer, owing to Mary's power rising up from the grave. Of course, there may be a logical explanation for that, as there is an opening in the grove of trees that allows the sun to shine down on the stone and warm it throughout the day. Perhaps some of the locals were too caught up in the legend to seek any scientific explanation for what they were convinced was true. In reality, the stone slab covering Mary's grave is a "wolf stone," which are designed to keep the animals from digging up bodies in a burial ground. Wolf stones were quite common in parts of New England and can still be found today. There are accounts from the town's church records that reveal that when the good folk of York left Sabbath services, they were more than once confronted with the gruesome spectacle of roaming hogs and cattle "well yoked and ringed as the law directs and allowed to go at large" rooting bodies up from fresh burials.

There is a fascinating drawing in the collection of the Old York Historical Society that was done in the 1830s of the burial ground. The drawing by an older resident of York was based on his childhood memory of the burial ground, and actually shows the cemetery with multiple wolf stones on the graves. There is some discussion that as the cemetery became abandoned and disused, perhaps the locals would go in and remove the stones to be used as part of foundations and other structures, since the threat of rooting animals in an overgrown burial ground didn't seem an issue any longer.

In the book, *Ancient City of Gorgeana and Modern Town of York (Maine) from Its Earliest Settlement,* by George Alexander Emery, in 1894, there is a commentary on the burial of Mary Nasson arguing that she couldn't have been a witch because she died too young, and it was known that witches seldom or never marry. In addition, the passage goes on to say that "it would have been very doubtful, indeed, if the powers that were would have allowed, or even suffered, her burial in this grave-yard. If a witch, she would have been interred in 'the rough sands of the sea, at low-water mark, where the tide ebbs and flows twice in twenty-four hours,' or on a highway, at the junction of three roads."

Whether or not you choose to believe that Mary was a witch, there is a distinct possibility that she might be a ghost in the burial ground. There have been numerous accounts over the years that children would be pushed by Mary's ghost on the swings that were once across from the cemetery (now there is a parking lot in its place). She was described as a sweet spirit who could be seen crossing the street and disappearing behind her gravestone. There were even stories that bunches of wildflowers would be found in piles, left as gifts for the children along the stone wall. Perhaps Mary's spirit is trying to reveal herself as sweet and kindly—far from the rumors that have been passed down for two hundred years.

Another legend tells of a two-story house that stood near the burial ground before 1829 that was haunted by an "evil spirit" that had to be sent peacefully to the spirit world. The story goes on to say that when the ghost was cleared from the house, it would wander around the burial ground to invite others who had passed on to join the spirit in inhabiting the world of the living. According to the tale, many of the villagers had a difficult time believing this spirit existed in the cemetery—until they could actually see it for themselves.

The burial ground is also home to a wonderful grove of sassafras trees. These tall, sturdy trees are registered with the state of Maine, and each has a numbered silver tag. A rarity in New England, these trees provided the early settlers with a resource for making all sorts of tinctures and beverages. The bark, flowers, and leaves were used for making a variety of products. When the leaves of the tree are crushed, they produce a scent similar to that of lemons, which was also used for making tea. It is curious that these trees are thriving in this cemetery, with the decaying remains of the early settlers eternally serving as fertilizer.

Another notable stone provides the following warning:

JOHN BRAGDON a promising Youth, departed this life
June 19th 1744 in Ye 23d Year of his Age;
with some comfortable Hope in his Death,
after great Distress of Soul, & solemn
Warnings to young People,
not to put off their Repentance to a Death Bed.

The burial ground is also the final resting place of one of the most famous ministers in York during the seventeenth century, Reverend Samuel Moody. Father Moody had gained quite a reputation for his unusual manner of preaching and for the strange use of church funds. There are countless tales about his actions during his ministry in York. Many parishioners grew tired of his extensively long sermons and others were offended by the topic of his preaching. As they left the church, Father Moody would shout after them, "Come back, you graceless sinner, come back!" His sermons were so long that he actually hired people with "poking sticks" to walk among the pews to literally poke at anyone who might have fallen asleep or became inattentive. The minister was so bold as to follow some of the parishioners to the local taverns and alehouses and he would drag them out of the establishment, admonish them, and send them home to contemplate their manner of sins. For as zealous as he was, Reverend Samuel Moody was also very kind. In fact he gave away his wife's only pair of shoes from her bedside to a poor woman who came to the house one frosty winter morning barefoot. The haunting sounds of his sermons can still be heard today emanating from the old church to the grounds of the cemetery.

The Old York Burial ground is full of stories, eccentric characters, and even a ghost of an accused village witch. For the graveyard enthusiast this burial ground seems to have more than just legends to offer, as it truly is an amazing museum of gravestones, carvings, and intriguing people.

VERMONT

THE DEBTOR AND THE GRAVE

A straying, silent breeze came by
And bent red clover to the grass,
The clouds were slow across the sky,
Even time itself could hardly pass.
The fresh-cut grass lay in the sun,
And birds flew near to sing and stay
Where memories of lives long done
Were fixed in marble half grown gray.
Behind each stone, square-cut and cold,
Through all that day's unresting heat,
Edged with the sunshine's summer gold,
A long, cool shadow marked six feet.

—*"A New England Graveyard"*

A strange and unnatural burial custom was described in a book about the history of eastern Vermont. In 1785, Judge Thomas Chandler of Chester, Vermont, was imprisoned as a debtor and was awaiting his sentence when he died. His death led to an unusual circumstance.

During the eighteenth century it was believed that if the remains of a person who died in prison were removed by friends beyond the boundaries of the jail, they were regarded as accomplices in an "escape." Therefore, whatever sentence was imposed on the prisoner would be applied to those who had moved the body in order to satisfy the judgment. Another belief at the time regarding the burial of an imprisoned debtor was that anyone who buried the body would become regarded as the executioner, and an intermeddler of the debtor's estate and also be liable to his satisfy his sentence.

It was a perplexing issue: How could a Christian burial be given to Judge Chandler's remains without the responsibility of satisfying his debts? For several days the corpse remained unattended in the cell of the jail. Those who did not want to help solve the issue shunned the corpse and would not speak of it. Eventually the body began to decompose and had become so physically offensive it endangered the health of the prisoners confined in the jail. The jailer, Nathan Fisk, offered a solution that was quickly put into practice. He had discovered that by stretching the chain that confined the inmates he could reach the burial ground that was adjacent to the jail. A grave was then dug just outside of the graveyard fence, but within the jail-yard limits. Once the hole was dug with equal parts under the cemetery fence and the jail yard it was time to bury the body. In the silence of midnight the putrid, rotting corpse of once respected Judge Chandler was dumped into a crude box and placed in its final resting place by the jailer and his assistants. In the end, the law was not violated because he was buried within the jail limits, and beneath the consecrated soil of the old Westminster churchyard.

Vampire Graves in Vermont

A month I watched her dying, pale, pale as any rose
That drops its petals one by one and sweetens as it goes.
My life was darkened when at last her large eyes closed in death,
And I heard my own name whispered as she drew her parting breath;
Still, still was the heart of New England.

It was a woeful funeral the coming sabbath-day;
We bore her to the barren hill on which the graveyard lay,
And when the narrow grave was filled, and what we might was done,
Of all the stricken group around I was the loneliest one;
And drear are the hills of New England.

—Edmund Clarence Stedman, 1908, "The Lord's Day Gale"

The green mountain state has two curious stories that relate to vampire superstition, which caused graves to be opened and gruesome acts to be committed to the bodies of the deceased. The first incident happened in 1793 and took place in a town called Manchester, located in southern Vermont. Rachel Harris, described as a beautiful young woman, married Captain Isaac Burton. Although Rachel was in good health when she married, less than a year after her wedding day she became deathly ill and succumbed to consumption. Captain Burton remarried about a year after the death of Rachel. Hulda Powel was also in good health at the time of her marriage, although some say she was not as beautiful as Rachel. Within months of the marriage Hulda became ill as well, displaying the same symptoms as Rachel, coughing up blood, an ashen face and extended lethargy. The notion came to some of the family and friends that perhaps a vampire had killed Rachel and was now going after Hulda.

According to Judge John S. Pettibone, who was a Probate Judge and represented Vermont in the General Assembly from 1822 to 1842, wrote the following in a manuscript that is in the possession of the Manchester Historical Society:

> They were induced to believe that if the vitals of the first wife could be consumed by being burned in a charcoal fire it would effect a cure of the sick second wife. Such was the strange delusion that they disinterred the first wife who had been buried about three years. They took out the liver, heart, and lungs, what remained of them, and burned them to ashes on the blacksmith's forge of Jacob Mead. Timothy Mead officiated at the altar in the sacrifice to the Demon Vampire who it was believed was still sucking the blood of the then living wife of Captain Burton. It was the month of February and good sleighing. Such was the excitement that from five hundred to one thousand people were present. This account was furnished me by an eye witness of the transaction.

Despite the actions taken on the body of Rachel, Hulda died on September 6, 1793.

Isaac Burton's grave can be found today in the scenic Dellwood Cemetery in Manchester, he is buried with his fourth wife, Dency Raymond. The unmarked grave of Rachel is believed to be somewhere on the village green where the courthouse can be found today.

The other well known story of vampirism happened in the town of Woodstock, located in central Vermont. The account of events has appeared in several publications including *The Journal of American Folklore* and later in the *Boston Transcript*. This story took place in the 1830s.

According to the story, a man by the name of Corwin had died from consumption and his body was buried in the Cushing cemetery. Soon after Corwin's death his brother became very ill, and it was determined that he had also been stricken with consumption. Some people believed that perhaps the dead brother was rising from the grave and coming back for fresh blood.

To be certain the town disinterred the body of the dead Corwin brother and examined his heart. According to the town's leading Physician, Doctor Joseph Gallup, the heart contained its victim's blood, although there still is a bit of speculation as to how he came to that determination. According to the Vermont newspaper *The Standard*, the heart was taken to the middle of Woodstock Green, where they kindled a fire under an iron pot, placed the heart inside and burned it until it was nothing but ashes. Some of the ashes were mixed with bull's blood and fed to the dying Corwin, hoping that the curse would be broken, and the blood elixir would save him. The ashes that were left in the pot were then buried under a seven-ton granite slab. Ten years later people who were digging at the site encountered a sulfurous smell and smoke spewing forth from the ground. Strangely there is no information as to whether the remaining Corwin brother lived after drinking the ghastly mix.

There are no gravestones in the Cushing cemetery that bear the Corwin name. Could it be that time and weather have worn away reminders of the past, hiding the dark deeds that happened back during the early nineteenth century? The seven ton granite slab from the town green is also missing. Town records do indicate these people truly did exist. Perhaps there has been enough digging into the past and this mystery is best left alone, as the bodies should have been.

Evergreen Cemetery, New Haven Vermont

Taphophobia is the fear of being buried alive. Translated from Greek, it literally means the "fear of graves." A usual place to find a depiction of this is in the Evergreen Cemetery located in a little county farm town called New Haven, among the rolling hills of Vermont. This gorgeous, well-maintained cemetery has one strange anomaly in it which harkens back to the days of Edgar Allen Poe's novel, *The Premature Burial.*

The grave of Dr. Timothy Clark Smith (1821–1893) stands out among the beautifully carved stones. Dr. Smith led a fascinating life that literally took him all around the world. He was also a schoolteacher, and served as a clerk to the Treasury Department. After obtaining his Doctor's degree in 1855, he became a surgeon in the Russian army. Later he served as United States consul to Russia in both Odessa and Galatz until 1883. Approximately ten years after his return to Vermont, Dr. Smith passed away on Halloween night.

The Vermont newspaper, the *Middlebury Register,* reported that Dr. Smith "died suddenly on Saturday morning at the Logan House [hotel] where he had been living. After breakfast, he walked out into the office and stood by the stove when stricken."

During the nineteenth century, many people feared being buried alive because of stories from all around the world of people who were presumed to be dead, and buried prematurely. Dr. Smith was afraid of sleeping sickness overtaking him and making him appear dead, when in fact, he'd still be living. Therefore, those in charge of his remains exercised precautions to prevent him from being buried alive.

First off, the burial was delayed for as long as possible, to make certain he was dead. During this time, Smith's burial vault was built and was overseen by his son, Harrison T.C. Smith, of Gilman, Iowa. The design of the vault offered stairs and a viewing window at the top of a glassed shaft so that Dr. Smith's interred body could look out and passers by could look in. A second room was built for Dr. Smith's wife, Catherine.

Dr. Smith's grave is near the front of the cemetery, rising up on a low hill. The locals say that upon looking into the window, you can still see the skeleton of Dr. Smith, and at his side, a hammer and chisel so that he could dig himself out of the grave if need be. It was also said that Dr. Smith was buried with a bell in his hand so he could ring it, should he wake from the dead. Viewing into the grave today is difficult due to the condensation that has built up in the window and the moss that appears to be growing on the inside corners of the window.

The burial ground is a beautiful place to explore, with the large receiving tomb still intact on the side of the hill at the edge of the cemetery. The gravestones in the burial ground are all in wonderful condition and offer up a variety of well-preserved carvings. However, the most fascinating grave in the cemetery is most certainly that of Dr. Smith, who was terrified of being buried alive.

PHOTOGRAPHY

Gravestones slope down the hill at Copps Hill Burial Ground. Strangely, many stones have been recovered in the basements of area houses.

Ancient stones crumble away in Hatfield, Massachusetts.

A curious black cat wanders the old burial ground in Exeter, New Hampshire.

The original town meetinghouse still stands at the front of the Harpswell, Maine, cemetery.

The setting autumn sun illuminates the stones in the burial ground located behind the Old Meeting house in Jaffrey, New Hampshire.

The gate and stonewall at the entrance to the cemetery in Harpswell. How many bodies have passed through to their final resting place?

The early November colors surround this roadside burial ground in Rye, New Hampshire.

A tree in a Salem, Massachusetts cemetery.

The autumn colors seem to set the scene ablaze in a Windsor, Vermont, graveyard.

This nineteenth-century hilltop burial ground located in Sandgate, Vermont, is largely forgotten about and quite overgrown. A variety of snakes curl around the bases of the stones, making a visit here a little unnerving.

Newport, Rhode Island, has a large variety of seventeenth- and eighteenth-century gravestones.

Burial Hill in Newburyport, Massachusetts, offers this fascinating epitaph.

A life-size angel stands over a grave in Chepachet, Rhode Island.

The willow and urn motif can be found throughout the churchyard cemetery in Arlington, Vermont.

An abandoned and quite haunted cemetery is hidden in the woods of Preston, Connecticut.

Sunset descends on a seaside cemetery in Stonington, Connecticut.

One of the oldest burial grounds in Maine, Old York Village is rumored to be quite haunted.

Does the spirit of Wizard Dimond still wander through the grave stones of Old Burial Hill in Marblehead?

The Hope Cemetery offers a variety of unique carvings, including the marriage bed of William and Gwendolyn Halvosa. Clad in pajamas, they sit up holding hands for eternity.

A large stone chair marks the Ross family plot at the Philips Heil cemetery. It is believed that the chair offers a resting place for the souls of the departed.

The grave of Robert Frost can be found in the very scenic Old First Church Graveyard in Bennington, Vermont.

This roadside cemetery in Nottingham, New Hampshire, is quickly being reclaimed by nature.

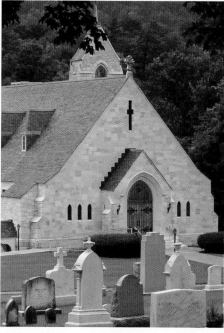

Located in New Castle, New Hampshire, the portrait gravestone for Abagail Frost depicts a variety of iconography, including an anchor and an angel carrying a crown.

The cemetery in Proctor, Vermont, as well as St. Dominic's Catholic Church, almost entirely feature white Vermont marble.

A gravestone for a Doctor in Simsbury, Connecticut, depicts a sun, moon, and a Mason's symbol.

Stonington Connecticut's oldest buying ground dates from 1650.

A poignant marble carving in Stonington, Connecticut, depicts an angel carrying two infants to heaven. An owl symbolizing wisdom and faithfulness is part of the carving.

In Mystic, Connecticut, a quaint epitaph reads, "Jane, Widow of Mr. George Denison, died May 11th, 1829 aged 98 years." At the time of her death, her children and their descendents were numbered at 350. To add to their happiness was her most ardent wish.

The hillside cemetery in Simsbury, Connecticut, contains a number of red sandstone grave markers.

Gravestones are seemingly being pulled into the ground by the overgrowth in Preston, Connecticut.

MASSACHUSETTS

A gravestone from 1708 in Salem, Massachusetts, depicts three skulls.

Tools of the gravedigger and a skeleton with a scythe can be found on a gravestone on Burial Hill in Newburyport, Massachusetts.

A gravestone from 1724 in Groveland, Massachusetts, depicts an angel with spider-like wings.

One of the oldest burial grounds in Massachusetts, the Ipswich Burial ground started in 1634.

Visitors to Old Burial Hill in Plymouth have described seeing specters walking amongst the gravestones.

Gravestones crowd the aisles at the Granary Burial ground in Boston, Massachusetts.

An eighteenth-century gravestone for a mother and her two children in Groton, Massachusetts.

The seventeenth-century Kings Chapel Burial Ground was Boston's only burial ground for thirty years.

Crowded gravestones in Ipswich lean in and out of the shadows

Mount Auburn in Cambridge, Massachusetts, was America's first garden-style cemetery established in 1831. The cemetery attracts over tens of thousands of visitors from all over the world.

The branches of trees reach across the rows of old tombstones in Lunenburg, Massachusetts.

Three eighteenth-century gravestones in Sunderland, Massachusetts, offer a fascinating glimpse into the local folk art style of gravestone carving.

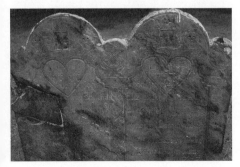

Four skulls can be found on the grave of Mr. and Mrs. White in Lunenburg, Massachusetts.

In a Hadley, Massachusetts, graveyard, an angel looks towards the heavens on this gravestone from 1792.

This stone carved by Nathaniel Phelps in 1777 stands in the Bridge Street cemetery in Northampton, Massachusetts.

Wellfleet, Massachusetts, offers a variety of gravestones with a winged-skull design.

A skeleton carries a "Death Dart" on a stone carving in Plymouth, Massachusetts.

Visitors seeking a glimpse of history are often drawn to the burial grounds in Salem, Massachusetts.

Table stones crumble a little more every year in the Old Deerfield Burial Ground.

A clock can be found on this gravestone from 1754 in the Old Deerfield Burial Ground.

A mother and her baby are depicted on this unusual stone in Deerfield, Massachusetts.

The wooden gates to the haunted cemetery in Princeton, Massachusetts, are rotting away.

Many people believe Old Burial Hill in Plymouth to be one of the most haunted places on Massachusetts southern coast.

The sign for the Old Burial Hill cemetery in Marblehead recounts the history of the area.

A stone from 1724 in the Pentucket Burial Ground.

Copps Hill Burial Ground in Boston was the scene of grisly events during the 1800s.

In Cambridge, Massachusetts, a gravestone from 1691 depicts "Death Imps," who were thought to be bringers of death.

A grave for five children who died in 1778 in Lexington, Massachusetts.

An angel lifts an infant out of a coffin on this nineteenth-century stone at the Mount Auburn Cemetery in Cambridge, Massachusetts.

The grave of Martha Keyes in Princeton, Massachusetts.

The inviting arched gates of a cemetery in Ipswich, Massachusetts, reads, "Blessed are the dead who die in the Lord."

New Hampshire

Established in 1735, the old burial ground in Amherst, New Hampshire, is located behind the Town Hall. Among the accidental deaths of those buried here are an unnamed child of Henry Howard who died from drinking a "large quantity of rum" in May of 1805. In May of 1836, according to town records, six burial lots were sold for the sum of fifty cents each.

The Point of Graves contains grave markers carved by John Homer of Boston, Massachusetts. Homer's dramatic stones are easily identified by his signature style of bold skulls and crossbones.

The Valley Cemetery in Manchester, New Hampshire, is currently undergoing a major restoration. Visitors to the cemetery claim to have heard disembodied voices throughout the grounds.

Located in Dover, New Hampshire, the gravestone for Mr. Joseph Belknap, dated 1797, offers a stylistic interpretation of a winged skull.

The image of an angel (with tiny feet) breaking off a budding flower can be found on the grave of nineteen-year-old Joanna Janvrin in Exeter, New Hampshire, who passed away in 1847. The symbolism of the breaking flower indicates a life cut short.

These three stones in Pine Grove cemetery in Hampton, New Hampshire, depict winged skulls (soul effigies) from 1715 and 1717. On top of one of the skulls is an hourglass representing the passage of time. The wings on the other two skulls present the heart as being risen up (being made) victorious over death.

Elizabeth Pierce's gravestone, located at the Point of Graves cemetery in Portsmouth, New Hampshire. She is believed to be one of the most active spirits on the grounds.

Gravestones at the Point of Graves in Portsmouth always warrant a closer look. Note the wings forming the shape of a heart.

The gravestone for Lydia Worcester at the Old Churchyard Cemetery in Hollis, New Hampshire, depicts two skulls and a coffin within a coffin. The epitaph reveals that Lydia died in childbirth. Lydia and her newborn are buried in this plot.

Mary's spirit is said to rise up from her grave every Halloween night as she makes her way across town to the house she used to live in.

The South Cemetery in Portsmouth, New Hampshire, has been a burial ground since the eighteenth century. However, it was also one of the sites of the town gallows.

RHODE ISLAND

The Belmont family plot in Newport, Rhode Island, seems more fitting in a museum with life-size Greek Goddesses and ornate stonework.

An unusual stone can be found in Newport, Rhode Island, that depicts the sad mortality rate of children. Three boys and three girls of the Langley family are buried beneath one long stone depicting six cherubs.

MAINE

The Old Fields graveyard in Berwick, Maine, is hidden in the woods and is overgrown with wildflowers during the summer.

A winter blanket covers the ground in the Village Cemetery in Fryeburg, Maine.

Angels were a common image used on gravestones in the mid-to-late eighteenth century. These angels can be found in a Kennebunk, Maine, churchyard.

In the Congregational Church Burial ground in Kittery, Maine, is a fascinating stone that depicts a ship with tattered sails crashing into an island and one of the passengers throwing their hands up in the air. The epitaph reads:

Brig 'Hattie Eaton'
W.I. to Boston
Cast away on Gerrish
Island Mch 21, 1876
Crew of 8 white and
negro and 1 stowaway,
Near this stone lie six
bodies never claimed.

The portrait stone for Mary Nasson was carved by the Lamson family of stone carvers in Boston, Massachusetts.

The Eastern Cemetery in Portland has been a victim of vandalism over the past thirty years.

Plain and simple stones mark the graves in a haunted and nearly forgotten cemetery in New Gloucester, Maine.

A simple grave marker with a winged skull in the Old York Burial grounds declares that Joseph Sayword was an Elder in the community.

One of the oldest surviving gravestones in the Eastern Cemetery dates from 1769 and depicts a winged skull with a keyhole-shaped nose.

VERMONT

Two pyramids with curious inscriptions can be found in the Hope Cemetery. One pyramid quotes the Book of Revelations and the other is inscribed, "If you met Daniel Morrell Vrooman 9-6-1938 and forgot him, you have lost nothing. But if you met Jesus Christ and forgot him you have lost everything."

A collection of gravestones carved by Zerubabbel Collins stands in the old cemetery located in Shaftsbury, Vermont.

Elia Corti's monument in the Hope Cemetery was cut from a single piece of granite by the brother of the deceased. The carved details of the clothing and the tools of the granite trade almost bring this figure to life.

The detailed sculpture of Margaret Pitkin in Montpelier, Vermont, attracts well-wishing visitors.

The Green Mount cemetery in Montpelier, Vermont, offers the unique "Stairs to Nowhere" sculpture. Carved from a rock ledge at the front of the cemetery, the symbolism depicts the soul's ascent to heaven or the afterlife.

Located in Bennington, Vermont, the gravestone of William Ellery Channing reads:

In this quiet village among the hills
William Ellery Channing
Apostle of faith and freedom
Died at sunset
October 2, 1842

STONES

Epitaphs

Because I could not stop for Death,
He kindly stopped for me.
The carriage held but just ourselves,
And immortality.

—Emily Dickinson

Epitaph – noun; Medieval Latin; 14th century 1 : an inscription on or at a tomb or a grave in memory of the one buried there 2 : a brief statement commemorating or epitomizing a deceased person or something past.
—Merriam-Webster Dictionary

For those curious visitors to cemeteries that are truly looking for the voice of the dead, one should ponder the final words that remain of the departed by reading their epitaphs. Throughout the shaded avenues of graveyards there are many of these final words carved in stone. Many stone carvers would actually charge by the letter, and one can only imagine the costs of some of the more wordy selections. Evidently there must have been much to say about the departed in many instances. Epitaphs served many purposes: they memorialized the dead, expressed the immediate feeling of loss experienced by the living, and connected the living to the dead. Some epitaphs were very good at recreating a person's entire life or death. Others could say so much about the person with so few words. Many earlier epitaphs had a way of scaring the passerby with bold remarks of death, causing the visitor to contemplate their own existence on earth. The eternal absence caused by death brought about the attempt to communicate with the dead. Epitaphs were a dialogue, visualizations of the dead and an attempt to connect them with the Word of God.

Epitaphs are indeed voices from the past, a haunting reminder that our cemeteries were filled with everyone from "A loving mother dear" to a "Patriot of the American Revolution." Many epitaphs mark tragic events that shaped the growth of our nation. While it may only take a few minutes to read the words carved on a gravestone, it took a lifetime for someone to live them. Brush back the dirt, push aside the grass, and read the memories of lives gone past, and you will find that the person buried there had something to say. A burial ground's ghostly spirits are one way to connect with the souls that have gone before us ... their epitaphs are another.

There are countless gravestones throughout New England, and here is just a sampling of some of their stories.

NEWPORT, RHODE ISLAND

Here lieth entombed the body of
Abagail, wife of Mr. George Wanton
Who dies May 12th 1726 in the 28th year of her age,
having left five pledges of her love.
If tears alas could speak a husband's woe
My verse would steight in plantif numbers flow;
Or if so great a loss deplored in vain
Could solace so my throbbing heart from pain
Then would I, oh sad consolation chuse
To soothe my cureless grief a private muse;
But since thy well known piety demons
A publick monument at they George's hands
O Abagail I dedicate this tomb to the
Thou dearest half of poor forsaken me.

In Memory of Mrs. Ann the wife of Captain Johnathan Clarke
Who resign'd this transitory life
The 29th of January 1764
In the 61 year of her Age.

This stone is erected to the Memory of Mr. William Rogers,
Merch.
Who departed this life on the 1st of October 1772, AE at 63
In Him did thine the affectionate Husband,
Tender Parent & Kind Master.
Remember Lord our immortal state
How frail our life, how mort the date
Where is the man that draws his breath
Safe from disease, secure form death.

SOUTH KINGSTOWN, RHODE ISLAND

There is an unusual marker that actually marks the spot of a
murder rather than a grave on Tower Hill Road in South Kingstown,
Rhode Island. This four-foot granite block commemorates the fate
of William Jackson, on a January night in 1751:

East side

This pillar is erected to the memory of William Jackson of
Virginia, who was murdered upon this spot by ship captain
Thomas Carter of Newport, Rhode Island, who, having been ship-
wrecked, and rendered penniless thereby, and being overtaken by
Mr. Jackson, who, also being on his way north, furnished him with
money and use of a horse on the way; having arrived at the point
that is indicated by this pillar, Carter there robbed and ...

North side

... murdered his kind and confiding benefactor with a dagger,
about the hour of midnight of Jan. first, 1751, was tried and
convicted of his crime at the village of Tower Hill on April 4th,
1751, and was hung in chains upon a gibbet May 10th, 1751, at
the eastern foot of the public highway where the shrieking—as it
were—of its chains, &c., during boisterous winds at night, were
the terror of many persons who lived ...

West side

… thereto, or passed thereby, one of these being the late Governor George Brown of Boston Neck, who told this writer that such had been his case when a youth, while on his way to the residence of College Tom Hazard that he visited every week. It appears that Carter threw Jackson in the "Narrow River" at the time he committed this murder, and that a negro found him therein, and near the abovementioned gibbet. A wayside inn-keeper,…

South side

… Mrs. Nash, who lived about ten miles westward from Tower Hill, happening to be at this village at the time this body was found, she recognized it as being that of Jackson, by means of a button she had sewn upon his vest only a few hours before he left her house, and that Captain Carter was with him. Carter was therefore arrested, tried, and condemned, and executed accordingly. (Erected by) Joseph Peace Hazard. 1889.

PAWTUCKET, RHODE ISLAND

Sacred to the memory of Capt. John George Curien,
Who died August 16th, 1824, in the ninety-first year of his age.
He crossed the raging ocean, This country for to save,
Twas France that gave him birth, And America a grave.

PROVIDENCE, RHODE ISLAND

Howard Phillips
Lovecraft
AUGUST 20, 1890,
MARCH 15, 1937.
"I am Providence"

PORTSMOUTH, NEW HAMPSHIRE

Hannah, Widow of Dr. Joshua, d. April 24, 1805, a. 71.
A pious, cheerful, rational Christian, possessing an active and
intelligent
mind, much of her time was employed in literary pursuits and
her acquirements were manifested with that female diffidence
which made her conversation pleasing to men of science.
Sacred to the Memory of Captain Joshua Lang Huntress
Who died Dec., 21, 1802
AE 50
He bore a lingering sickness with patience and
Met the King of terrors with a smile.

GILMANTON, NEW HAMPSHIRE

In Memory of Joseph Salter, aged 17 years,
son of Capt. Richard Salter of Portsmouth, N. H.,
the beloved youth ascended in' the flames of a mansion house on
yonder hill Saturday
morning, Feb. 6, 1802 at 4 o'clock A. M.
Glorify ye the Lord in the Fires. Isaiah 24, 5.
As from Manoah's rock in ancient days
Uprose the Angel from surrounding blaze
Thus rose the spirit of the son of Love
On fiery pinneons (sic) to the realms above.

WOBURN, MASSACHUSETTS

In Memory of Mr. Joshua Richardson, who died July 14, 1807,
Aged 30 years.
This sudden death was occasioned by the fall
Of a house frame, to the disappointment &
Grief of his father, brothers, sisters, and a
Virtuous female whom he anticipated
For the partner of his life.

There are many who are buried in the Second Burial Ground of Woburn, who perished on July 14, 1807, when the frame of the three-story Clapp mansion collapsed. Witnessed by many of the town who came out to see this historic house raising, it was a catastrophe that lingered in the community for many years. Major Jeremiah Clapp, Esq., was a man of wealth and importance, and thus the building of his dwelling, larger than most homes for miles around, commanded an unusual attendance of visitors and supporters. Two sides of the mansion were not braced strongly, and when the timbers for the crown roof were being placed, the frame leaned to the west. Shortly thereafter the witnesses at the scene stood shocked when the structure came crashing down, crushing several men who were inside. The screams of agony that broke the air and over thirty of the strongest men in town were injured with nearly a half dozen being killed. The gravestones of Richardson, Wright, and Parker are found in the Second Burying Ground, adorned with epitaphs uniquely descriptive of their virtues, and lament the loss of their lives in the disaster.

GORHAM, MAINE

Prince
A slave, whom the first William McLellan of Gorham
bought in Portland, Me.
and paid for in Shooks.
Prince drove the team to draw them.
He ran away and enlisted on Capt. Manley's Privateer
and was discharged in Boston,
came back, was freed, given
10 acres of land, and a pension.
Died 1829, over 100 y's old.
His Wives
Dinah died 1800.
Chloe died 1827.

GREAT CRANBERRY ISLAND, MAINE

CHARLES HARDING
DIED
Oct. 27, 1883
AE.63yrs.3mos.
My husband how fondly shall thy memory
Be shrined within the chambers of my heart
Thy virtuous worth was only known to me
And I can feel how sad it is to part

KITTERY, MAINE

In this dark, silent Mansion of the Dead,
A lovely Mother, and sweet Babe, are laid.
Of ev'ry Virtue of her Sex possest,
She charm'd the World, and made a Husband blest.
Of such a Wife, O righteous Heaven, bereft,
What joy for me, what joy on Earth, is left?
Still, from my inmost Soul, the Groans arise,

Still flow the Sorrows, ceaseless from my Eyes.
But why these Sorrows, so profusely shed?
They may add to but ne'er can raise the Dead.
I soon shall follow the same dreary Way,
That leads, and opens, to the Coasts of Day,
There clasp them both, upon the happy Shore,
And Bliss shall join, nor Death shall part us more.

Mary Chauncy, Wife of Charles Chauncy, and Daughter to the
Honble
Richard Cutt Esqr. died April 23d. 1758, in the 24th. Year of her
Age, with
her Infant Son Charles Chauncy.

PERRY, MAINE

LORING Jeremiah, son of Isaac and Betsy LORING,
died May 19, 1864, ae 21 yrs.
Member of Co. K, 1st Me. Heavy Artillery, killed
in the Battle of the Wilderness.
"Rest in peace O patriot hero
With our country's glorious dead
Sleeping 'neath the soil made sacred
By the precious blood they shed."

ENFIELD, CONNECTICUT

Sacred to the memory of Dea. Joseph Kingsbury, who died June
8th, 1806, aged 85
and 2 months.
Here lies a man, no one priz'd religion more,
The same our Fathers brought from Europe's shore,
A strict supporter of the good old ways
Of Puritans, in their most early days.

FAIRFIELD, CONNECTICUT

Here lies the Body of Thomas, Son
to Mr. Ebenezer & Mrs. Mary Bertram
he was Born February 22nd A. D. 1764 & Died
July 28th. A. D. 1764, Aged 5 Months & 6 Days.
Happy the Babe who privileged by Fate.
To Shorter Labour and a Lighter weight.
Receiv'd but yefterday the Gift of Breath
Order'd to morrow to Return to Death.

Here
lies interr'd the body
of Doctr. Thomas Him.
who died March 8th A. D.

1781. in the 36'".
Year of his Age.
tear
Some hearty friend shall drop his
On our dry Bones, and say,
Those once were strong as mine appear
And mine must be as they.

MILFORD, CONNECTICUT

Mary Fowler, 1792, age 24, Milford, CT

Molly tho' pleasant in her day
Was suddenly seized and went away
How soon she's ripe, how soon she's rotten
Laid in her grave and soon forgotten.

NEW HAVEN, CONNECTICUT

In Memory of
Samuel Barns Son of
Mr Samuel Barns & Mrs
Welthy Barns whose
Death was Occasion'd
by a Scald from a Tea pot
March 27th 1794 aged 7
Months
Suffer little Children Come unto
Me and forbid them not for of
Such is the Kingdom of Heaven

WREXHAM, CONNECTICUT

Under this tomb lyes interred Elihu Yale, of Plas Gronow, Esq.
born 5th of April, 1648, and dyed the 8th of July, 1721, aged 73 years.
Born in America, in Europe bred,

In Africa travel'd, and in Asia wed,
Where long he liv'd and thriv'd; at London dead.
Much good, some ill he did; so hope all even,
And that his soul through mercy's gone to heaven.
You that survive and read, take care
For this most certain exit to prepare,
For only the actions of the just
Smell sweet and blossom in the dust.

BRIDGEWATER, MASSACHUSETTS

Sacred to the memory of Mr. Ebenezer Noyes, died Aug.
1832, aged 37 years.
Come hither mortals, cast an eye
Then go your way prepare to die;
Come read this doom, for die you must,
One day like me return to dust.
Sacred to the, memory of Mrs. Susan Noyes and infant, wife
of Mr. Ebenezer Noyes, and dau. of Mr. Joseph Gannett and Mrs.
Ann, his wife; she died May 23, 1822, in her 25th year.
From creatures cease, a warning voice here cries,
They fade and vanish like the passing wave
With them the branch of hope they nourished dies,
And strews its blighted blossoms o'er the grave.

DEERFIELD, MASSACHUSETTS

Here lies the body of
Lieut. Mehuman Hinsdell
Died May 9, 1736 in the 63rd year of his age
He was the first male child born in this place &
Was twice captivated by the Indian Savages
Blessed are the Merciful, for they shall obtain Mercy.

IPSWICH, MASSACHUSETTS

Erected to the Memory of
Doctr. Joseph Manning
& Elizabeth his amiable Partner
in Life upwards of 46 years, who
died Jan. 30th 1779 in 71st year
of her age. He mourned her lose [sic]
until ye 8th of May 1784 and then
died in ye 80th year of his Age.
The toile of life and pangs of death are o'er
And care & pain & sickness are no more.

They both were plain and unaffected
in their Manners steady and Resalute
in their Conduct Humane, temperate,
Just & Bountiful.
Death can't disjoin whom Christ hath join'd in love,
Life leads to death, and death to life above.
In Heaven's a happier place frail things despise,
Live well to gain in futer life the prize.

LANCASTER, MASSACHUSETTS

In Memory of David Atherton Son of Mr. Amos &
Mrs. Elizabeth
Atherton who died July ye 4th 1769 in ye 14th Year of his Age.
"When this you see, Remember me."

LYNN, MASSACHUSETTS

Sacred to the Memory of four children of Timothy and Rachel
Munroe.

Timothy, Died June 24, 1827
Rachel E. died Sept. 16, 1828, aged 2 mos.

Rachel E. died Oct. 11, 1829, aged 3 months.
Mary J. died August 10, 1831, aged 11 months.
Oh cruel death, these little babes,
Thou hast taken from our love,
Yet we shall meet together soon
In brighter worlds above.

In Memory of Mrs. Eliza, wife of Mr. Edwin Newhall, and
Daughter of Mr. Benjamin and Mrs. Lydia Smith, who died
September 6, 1838, AEt. 23.
Also Adeline Augusta, their daughter, died September 21, 1838,
aged 10 months.
Think it not strange that budding flowers should die,
When death's rude hand broke down the parent tree,
Thou too with all thy budding hopes must lie
Where ruthless death hath laid thy child and me.

MARLBOROUGH, MASSACHUSETTS

Here lies Buried Body of Mr. William Barns
Aged 20 Years 2 Months, & 27 Days.
Here lies Buried Body of Mr. Aaron Barns
Aged 28 Years, & 10 Days.
They were awfully Drowned in the River June 18, 1773.
Behold Ye Mourners for the Dead,
In this cold grave we'v made our Bed;
And water prov'd our fatal End,
So Chill our Head, is mans best Friend.
Yea ! Man giveth up the Ghost, and where is he?

Note, it is a Very awful Consideration to think where they are
that have given up the Ghost, and where we shall be when we give it
up. The Soul is gone to the world of Spirits, into Eternity, to return
no more to this World. Oh! that we were wise, that we understood
this, that we would consider our latter End.

MONTAGUE, MASSACHUSETTS

In Memory of Mr. Elijah Bardwell
Who dies Janry 26th 1786 in ye 27th
Year of his Age having but a few days
Surviv'd ye fatal Night when he was
flung from his Horse & drawn by ye Stirrup
26 rods along ye path as appear'd by ye place
Where his hat was found & where he had
Spent ye whole following severe cold night
Treading ye Snow in a small circle...

NORTHFIELD, MASSACHUSETTS

John son of Mr Rufus and Mrs Asenath Stratton died
Aug 11 1790 aged J yr 4 mo and 17 days.
Death like an overflowing streams
Sweeps us away
Our life is a dream.
In memory of Mrs Tamar wife of Cap Ebenezer
Stratton who Died July 1, 1797 in the 74 year of
Her Age
Death comfortably ends
A well spent life.

PLYMOUTH, MASSACHUSETTS

James Jordan
Drowned in Smelt Pond,
June 25, 1837 aged 27 y'rs.
Buried on the day he was to have been married.

WELLESLEY, MASSACHUSETTS

SACRED to the memory of Elizabeth R. Ware who died
Aug. 1, 1847. Aged 21 yrs
erected as a token of respectful and
affectionate remembrance by her youthful friends.
Peace to thy spirit youthful maiden,
And peaceful be thy lowly rest,
With love's pure of ring we've come laden.
And with sad hearts by grief oppress'd,
To rear this stone and place this willow,
Where angels guard thy sweet repose.
And far above thy lowly pillow
We now have come to plant the rose.
Oft as the tree bears fruit in heaven.
May it here bloom to tell of thee.
The stone so pure, so spotless even,
The Hushing rose thine emblem be.

BRATTLEBORO, VERMONT

The Grave of Alanson D. Wood, who was killed instantly
on this river by the explosion of the Steamboat
Greenfield, May 18, 1840. Ae 30.

DANBY FOUR CORNERS, VERMONT

In Memory of four infants
Of Jacamiah & Mercy Palmer
Was born alive at one birth
& died Nov. 25, 1795.
Four twen infants they are dead
And laid in one silent grave
Christ took small infants in his arms
Such infants he will save.

FAIRHAVEN, VERMONT

In memory of Ezra Hamilton, who died Feb. 25th, 1810,
In the 77th year of his age.
Farewell, Farewell vain world
Farewell to thee,
For thou hast nothing
More to do with me.

FELCHVILLE, VERMONT

On the 31st of
August 1754
Capt James
Johnson had
a Daughter born
on this spot of
Ground being
Captivated with his whole Family
By the Indians

This is near the spot
That the Indians Encamped the
Night after they took Mr Johnson &
Family Mr Laberee & Farnsworth
August 30th 1754. And Mrs
Johnson was Delivered of her Child
Half a mile up this Brook.

When troubles near the Lord is kind,
He hears the Captives crys.
He an subdue the savage mind
And learn it sympathy.

NORWICH, VERMONT

In memory of Mr. Nathaniel Hatch who died with the
small pox at Charlestown N. H. July 3, 1776 aged (blank)
years. His bones were accidentally found in 1810 by men to
work on a turnpike between Charlestown and Walpole and
deposited at this place by the desire of his son Oliver Hatch
of this town.
Let not the dead forgotten He
Lest men forgit that they must die.

WESTMINSTER, VERMONT

In Memory of William French, Son to Mr. Nathaniel French :
Who
Was Shot at Westminster, March ye 17th, 1775, by the hands of
Cruel
Ministereal tools of Georg ye 3d in the Courthouse at a 11a
Clock at Night, in the 22d year of his Age. Here William French
his Body lies. For Murder his Blood for vengeance cries King
Georg the third his Tory crew that with a bawl his head Shot
threw For Liberty and his Country's God he Lost his Life his
Dearest blood.

GRAVESTONES: A VIRTUAL TOUR THROUGHOUT NEW ENGLAND

A shrewd gentlewoman, who kept a tavern in the town, was anxious to obtain two or three gravestones for the deceased members of her family, and to pay for these solemn commodities by taking the sculptor to board. Hereupon a fantasy arose in my mind of good Mr. Wigglesworth sitting down to dinner at a broad, flat tombstone, carving one of his own plump little marble cherubs, gnawing a pair of cross-bones, and drinking out of a hollow death's-head, or perhaps a lachrymatory* vase, or sepulchral urn, while his hostess's dead children waited on him at the ghastly banquet.

—Nathaniel Hawthorne, 1837, Chippings with a Chisel.

Gravestone carvings throughout New England are fascinating, and to some people, even frightening, especially when viewing these grim reminders of death. In this section of the book, we'll examine some of the interesting, notable, and unusual grave markers in New England, and note the changes in styles and carvings from the seventeenth century to the twentieth. It's amazing that some of these gravestones have stood in burial grounds throughout New England for over three hundred years; cemeteries really are outdoor museums of stone.

The earliest grave markers in New England were literally stones and boulders that were used to keep the dead from rising out of their graves. In these primitive times, people believed that if heavy rocks were placed on the grave sites of the deceased, they would not be able to climb out from underneath them. In some cases many of the markers were made from wood planks or rough stone, and

---

*   During the nineteenth century those mourning the loss of loved ones would collect their tears in bottles with special stoppers that allowed the tears to evaporate. When the tears had evaporated, the mourning period would end.

Providence, Rhode Island.

very often did not last long when exposed to the elements. As more burials occurred with the passing of time, the need arose to indicate on the markers either simple initials or names to identify the deceased.

Gradually these markers became more ornate reflecting early Puritan beliefs. These are evident in the first stone carvings, and reflect the beliefs that death was inevitable, and it was God's punishment for the original sin of Adam. They also believed that evil spirits and evil men occupied the earth, suffering from "utter and unalterable depravity." Children were shown corpses and were taught to fear death and that even their own parents would testify against them at the last judgment. The possibility of salvation was preached to all as a reward. The most glorious purpose to which a Puritan could live and work for during their lifetime was to "bring God's kingdom home." Some people in would be able to receive eternal salvation as a gift bestowed by God, but most faced eternal damnation. Hell was preached as a place of "unspeakable terrors."

During the seventeenth century, the settlers lived in a very simple, yet symbolic, world. Using the imagery that surrounded death and funerals at the time, gravestone carvers translated these beliefs using the ministers' sermons for inspiration. This imagery and iconography became one of New England's first folk art forms. A variety of skulls, crossed bones, winged hourglasses, pick axes, and shovels were just a few of the common symbols carved on the earliest gravestones in Puritan times. Without words, these symbols alone were identifiable images understood by the people. The belief was that as people passed by the burial grounds and saw these very stark reminders of death, they would be moved to ponder their own existences on earth. Puritans who regarded death

1690 Wolf Stone, Stonington, Connecticut.

as God's punishment for sins would often tremble with fear on their deathbeds, afraid that they might suffer eternal damnation in hell. Some stonecutters, however, went beyond the use of individual symbols and carved dramatic scenes of death imps carrying coffins away. Gravestone images depicted literal stories in stone, communicating moral lessons or spiritual truths. Not only were these gravestones memorials of the dead, they were messages to the living.

Early graveyards in New England seem to offer no particular logic as to how the bodies were arranged, and there was obviously no thought put towards visitors coming to spend time in the cemeteries, wander about, and contemplate the existence of the departed. Graveyards during the seventeenth and early eighteenth century were simply places to bury the dead, and this often led to the overcrowding of many of the first cemeteries. Bodies would be placed side by side, sometimes with rather shallow burial plots to maximize the space in the graveyard. In some cases extreme weather exposed coffins, prompting the remains to be re-interred deeper into the ground. In many rural towns, people chose to be buried right on their own property, and there are countless small family plots throughout every corner of New England. In towns such as York and Kittery, Maine, there are approximately three hundred family plots, while there are few major graveyards.

Headstones with footstones were first used in the seventeenth century throughout many of New England first cemeteries. The reason for these types of grave markings was the thought that people

Watertown, Massachusetts.

were laid to rest as if buried in their beds, and their bodies would be laid with their heads at the headboard, or the taller stone, and their feet at the footboard, the smaller stone. The headstones and the footstones commonly faced outwards and away from each other, so if you were to walk around the grave, they would be visible from the outside. And if you stand between them, you are right over the buried body. The footstones often bore initials of the deceased and similar designs as the headstones. The stones were typically made of the same material and were often of similar shape. Over the years, due to the shifting of the cemeteries, along with neglect

A headstone and matching footstone in Hatfield, Massachusetts.

and vandalism, a lot of footstones have gone missing or have been displaced to other parts of the cemeteries. Still, there are many burial grounds throughout New England where the stones still stand in their original configuration.

To outline the more basic stages in the development of gravestone styles in New England during the seventeenth through early nineteenth centuries, imagery consisted of an early "death's head" or "winged skull" style (late 1600s through circa 1790), which gave way over time to a "cherub's head" style (circa 1760 through 1810). This period of time was also known as the Great Awakening, which was an intense religious revival that swept the American colonies beginning in the 1720s, when attitudes toward death finally began to change. Where, in the seventeenth century, children were told to fear death, they were increasingly told in the eighteenth century to look forward to death as a reunion with God and their deceased relatives. Adults, in turn, were increasingly promised that a life of active piety assured salvation. Angels represented a belief in the resurrection and the peaceful ascent of the spirit into heaven. Many carvings would actually represent the deceased as an angelic figure ascending to heaven. Other versions depict angels carrying the departed soul. Soon after the resurrection shift, stone carvings began to depict more and more of the "urn and willow" style carvings (circa 1770 through mid 1800s). The urn and willow style of carving had its own belief system as well. The urns harkened back thousands of years to an unusual belief that had to do with the physical burial of the body. Urns were once used to store the

Barre, Vermont.

vital organs of the body after death for the resurrection. The vital organs consisted of the heart and lungs. Strangely, the brain was not considered a vital organ, and was disposed of. Often in Egypt when

Concord, New Hampshire.

the pyramid tombs of the Pharaohs were opened, these urns were discovered serving that purpose. The weeping willow was a symbol of everlasting life, for the belief was that if you were to cut the branches off of a willow tree, the tree would still continue to grow. These carvings typically depicted the tree bent over the urn, also a symbol of mourning. Gateposts also became common symbols on the grave markers to depict passing through the gates to the other side. Many grave markers had tall columns pointing skyward, symbolizing the ascension into heaven.

The date ranges of these changes shifts, and the character of developments within each of these stages varies from locality to locality within New England.

Moving into the nineteenth century, gravestones began to depict more ornate flowers, fingers pointing skyward, crowns, shafts of wheat, and other images suggesting successful life or victory over death. Sleeping lambs were commonly carved on the graves of children as a reminder of their innocence. Taking queues from the Victorian movement, cemeteries began to evolve into places where people were encouraged to visit and spend a leisurely afternoon. With beautiful tree-lined lanes and bushes of fragrant flowers, graveyards became destinations to take a romantic outing or have a picnic. Postcards were even developed depicting park-like graveyards with gazebos and ponds to visit. These garden-style cemeteries were popular recreation destinations during these times. During the twentieth century, gravestone styles shifted again. Epitaphs became simpler, and hand-carved stones became more of a rarity.

Today, there are a variety of burial grounds throughout New England and each offers a unique landscape and history. The gravestones all tell their own tale of those who had passed this way before us, and their reminders stand in these places that are more than worthy of exploration and appreciation.

Wilton, New Hampshire.

SUPERSTITIONS

SUPERSTITIONS

This life is a fleeting breath,
And whither and how shall I go,
When I wander away with Death
By a path that I do not know?

—*Louise Chandler Moulton, "When I wander away with death"*

There are numerous old superstitions throughout New England that deal with death and cemeteries. Some are amusing while others are quite unusual. Most of these early practices and customs that related to the burial of the dead have been long forgotten to the pages of dusty old books, town records, and genealogy records. This section highlights superstitious stories found in every section of New England.

EAST TO WEST AND THE DAY OF JUDGMENT

In the early Colonial days it was a custom to make the graves due east and west, and the body was placed in the grave with feet to the east. This custom was a vestige of the belief that on Judgment Day, when the Judge would appear in the eastern sky seated on a great white throne and the trumpets sounded, the graves would open and the dead would emerge in the same mortal form that they possessed at death. Hence, by being buried with feet to the east, the body, when it rose, should come upon its feet facing the great throne, and then stand straight and still until it had been judged and sentence passed upon it.

Another custom related to the preparations of the burial ground was to appoint some prominent place for the burial of persons related to the management of public affairs. This place extended north and south, so that the graves made in it should reach east and west. These important folk were buried in the cemetery side by side, with feet to the east in the same manner as others. On Judgment Day, those officials would rise up together, standing side by side, and would be judged collectively upon their official acts, as well as individually upon their characteristics.

THE BREATH OF DEATH

In 1885, the Division of Vital Statistics in Maine maintained by the State Board of Health recorded that a diphtheria epidemic was becoming quite prevalent. It was said that even during funerals the disease was spreading. Diphtheria attacks the throat and nose, and in more serious cases, it can attack the nerves and heart. Complications from diphtheria include paralysis, heart failure, blood disorders, and, in many cases, death.

It was recorded that at the burial of a young man who died from diphtheria, as the coffin was lowered into the grave, the lid came off. Two people in attendance who put the coffin lid back on were taken with this disease shortly after and both died. Several other persons who were at the burial took the disease soon after; of these, some recovered and some died. It was believed that by coming in close contact with the dead body, the air around it still contained the disease, which could be breathed in by those who were living.

THE GHOSTLY CURIOSITY OF COLONEL KNAPP, NEW HAMPSHIRE

There is a great story about a brave theatre critic by the name of Colonel Knapp who had visited a small village somewhere in New Hampshire in the early nineteenth century. Colonel Knapp seemed quite fascinated with ghosts, and he had always hoped for the opportunity to see if he could make contact with the other side.

In this small town the Colonel knew of one family who told stories of a ghost that visited the old burial ground every midnight. They seemed especially intrigued with the ghost story, as they had lost one of their daughters recently, and they had hoped to learn of her fate on the other side. Fascinated, the Colonel set out to see this ghost for himself. The Colonel arrived in town late that evening, and in the dark he headed for the cemetery in eager anticipation of seeing this ghost. After a few hours the Colonel laid down in front of a gravestone, where he gradually fell asleep. The ground where the curious Colonel lain down was damp and the stone and the ground seemed to be sinking around him. He awoke to find a woman in a white dress standing over him with a sorrowful look on her face. When the Colonel stood up, the specter in the white dress ran away, and he followed her. She disappeared right into his friend's house.

The very next morning the Colonel paid his friends a visit. A woman came down the stairs of the house and began to weep uncontrollably at the sight of the Colonel standing before her. She declared that she had a premonition of the Colonel lying in his grave in the local cemetery. Colonel Knapp realized that this was the woman who had showed at the gravesite in the darkened hour of night. After much discussion he found out that she was a chronic sleepwalker and she would often wander to the burial ground to stop at the grave of her deceased sister—coincidently the same grave that the Colonel had fallen asleep on. The woman soon sought help for her disorder and the ghost in this graveyard was never seen again. As for Colonel Knapp, he continued to seek out the existence of ghosts, however, not in this little village.

Burial Customs of "Number 5"

Hopkinton, New Hampshire, was first granted as a settlement simply known as "Number 5" in 1735. Incorporated as a town in 1765, it is situated just outside of Concord, the state capital. In 1890, the customs of the "disposal of the dead" from the town were chronicled by Charles Chase Lord. He explained that the coffins were made by the local carpenter, who didn't always have a coffin on hand in case of an emergency. The bodies were crudely wrapped in a sheet, and a window of glass was built into the coffin where the face would be visible for the mourners to peer in at. When services were complete, a piece of wood was screwed over the glass as a permanent obstruction to prepare the body for burial. A black cloth would be draped over the coffin and would be removed at the graveside. The cloth, known as a "pall," was owned by the town and used for countless interments. Some of the earliest grave markers were described as being made out of un-hewn rock with two simple initials, which were placed on Putney Hill by the early settlers. As the prosperity grew in the town, people could begin purchasing gravestones, and thus the graveyard on the hill expanded.

THE EARLY USE OF BURIAL GROUNDS IN PROVIDENCE, RHODE ISLAND

In 1700, burial customs changed in the city of Providence, Rhode Island. Up until that time, the early settlers had their own burial grounds as family plots on their property in the plantation. Other colonies were beginning to use churchyards, common burial grounds, and meetinghouse graveyards. The burying of the dead became more community oriented as opposed to being individually handled by families. With the expanding population and rising property values, there was a need for a common burying place. A parcel to the north of town was set aside for "a training field, burying ground, and other public uses." The cemetery got a boost in occupancy when Benefit Street (the back street of Colonial Providence), which had grown from a series of paths winding through backyards, was widened and straightened during the mid eighteenth century. At that time many of the early family plots were added to the community and moved from their original locations to the North Burial Ground to become part of the general population's resting place.

SPECTERS AND SKELETONS IN THE GRAVEYARD

Between Keene and Concord is the little country town of Antrim, New Hampshire. Settled in 1741, it was named for County Antrim in Ireland which was the native home of the land's owner, Philip Riley. Superstitions and burial customs intertwined into the lives of the early settlers of the town. One belief was if a corpse were kept unburied over the Sabbath, another death would occur in the town before the week was out. If a dead body were carried out of the house head first, there would be another death in the family before the next year had passed. If twice there were raps on the door, and when the door opened to reveal no one there, it was considered a sure warning of speedy death in that house. Dreams also had superstitious meanings, both good and bad. With the common saying, "Saturday night's dream, Sunday morning told, was sure to come to pass before a week old." There was a strong belief in fortune telling, as well.

Tales of haunted houses abounded, and it was even said that many in the town could not even be hired to venture into these spooky abodes. Ghosts were said to regularly appear in the town. Children were frightened into good behavior by their parents with the stories of warlocks, witches, bogles, hags, and beings of the darkest reaches of night. Many stories focused on cemeteries, which were said to have been inhabited by the most fearsome of spirits. If someone had found themself lost in the graveyard being chased by skeletons and the specters of death, they were told to run to the nearest stream, of which Antrim had many. Once safely across the waters, one would be out of harm's way, for the belief was that these undead creatures would not cross running water.

Meetinghouse Road in Antrim is a long, steep drive through the woods. Along this road is the old Meetinghouse cemetery, the oldest burial ground in town. Secluded and quiet, the burial ground is rather simple, and is surrounded by an old stone wall. Walking the area it is immediately noticeable how many graves date from the summer of 1800. A dysentery epidemic killed more than 60 of the town's children, all under the age of 12. Some visitors to the graves claim they have felt small hands clutching their hands, as if the children's spirits are searching for comfort.

DEAD ON THE TIDE

An old legend from Cape Cod ties the dead with the urges of the sea. The belief was that people believed a sick man could not die until the ebb tide began to run. Those who stood vigil over sick beds would anxiously note the change of the tides, and if the patient lived until the flood set in again, he would live until the next ebb. The superstition spread out to other coastal localities in New England. The legend was even immortalized by the words of Charles Dickens in the *Death of Barkis*:

> "People can't die, along the coast," said Mr. Peggotty, "except when the tide's pretty nigh out. They can't be born, unless it's pretty nigh in—not properly born, till flood. He's a going out with the tide. Its ebb at half after three, slack water half an hour. If he lives till it turns, he'll hold his own till past the flood, and go out with the next tide." We remained there, watching him, a long time—hours.

FOLLOW ME TO THE GRAVE

A long-standing custom in connection with the burial of the dead lasted well into the nineteenth century. The custom of carrying the dead feet first out the front door of the home was practiced throughout New England. This tradition was based on the belief that the spirit of the deceased could still beckon others to follow it to death, and would seek to return to the place where the living had resided. The corpse was carried feet first so that it could not see the door through which it had been taken out, or the route along which it had been carried to the grave, and therefore, not return.

WATCHING OVER THE DEAD

One of the most curious of the old-time New England superstitions was the custom of requiring young couples to watch the recently deceased corpse overnight. The association of the hopes of marriage with the silent vigil was quite poetic, and it ended somewhere in the nineteenth century. The social conscience placed an obligation to the dead, believing that they should not be left alone at night. In the earliest days of this custom, the solemn watchers were old men and women, deacons, and selectmen. However, as the colonies grew, engaged and honest lovers with strong morals were frequently selected for these long vigils in the hours of darkness. Disturbing and frightful were many of the stories that were relayed in villages of lovers who were troubled during such depressing duties by cats, owls, mysterious noises, and spectral visions.

RING OF DEATH

Funerary rings were often given at funerals in seventeenth- and eighteenth-century New England. Mourning rings, as remembrances of those loved ones who have preceded us to the land of spirits, were always cherished by families and passed down as an heirloom for generations. These rings were typically given to relatives and the wealthy and prominent people in the community. Doctor Samuel Buxton of Salem, Massachusetts, died in 1758 at the age of eighty-one, and left a tankard full of mourning rings that he had received at funerals over the years. In 1738, at one Boston funeral, over two hundred rings were given away to the mourners in attendance. People looked forward to receiving a funeral ring upon the death of a friend. There are many entries in old New England journals and books that characterize the experience of receiving a ring. Some recorded entries read, "Made a ring at a funeral," "A death's head ring made at the funeral of […]" and "Lost a ring—by not attending a funeral."

Mourning rings were usually made of gold, and were often beautifully enameled in black, sepia, or white. The rings often bore detailed images of skeletons, coffins, skulls, or urns often mirroring the imagery that was carved onto the gravestones. Some funeral rings bore a family crest in black enamel. Many were inscribed with mottoes such as, "death parts united hearts," "prepared be to follow me," and "death conquers all." Some rings featured intricate flowers, and others had the image of a snake swallowing its tail. Many more elaborate rings held framed locks of hair of the deceased, and were often worn by those who had lost a child, or by women. The hair would be either braided within the ring, or used as part of the images themselves—taking the form of trees, drapes, or flowers. Seed pearls were used as accents in mourning rings to symbolize tears.

When mourning rings were lost, often advertisements were printed in the local newspaper to assist in having them returned. A newspaper in Boston dated October 30, 1742, contained the advertisement, "Mourning ring lost with the Posy Virtue & Love is From Above." An advertisement from the *Boston Evening Post* read, "Escaped unluckily from me A Large Gold ring, a Little Key; The Ring had Death engraved upon it; The Owners Name inscribed within it; Who finds and brings the same to me Shall generously rewarded be."

Goldsmiths always kept a full stock of mourning rings on hand. "Deaths Heads Rings" and "Burying Rings" appear in many old newspaper advertisements. The rings would be engraved with the name or initials of the dead person, and the date of his death; this custom was called fashioning. There is also evidence in antique letters and bills that orders were sent by bereaved ones to friends who lived far away to purchase and wear mourning rings in memory of the dead, and to send the bills to the family.

A wonderful assortment of mourning rings is in the collection of the Peabody Essex Museum in Salem, Massachusetts. Over one hundred years ago the Institute even went so far as to put together a lengthy list of such rings that had existed in Salem.

A Toast to Death

At the funeral of Mrs. Mary Norton, widow of John Norton, one of the ministers of the first church in Boston, in 1678, it was recorded in probate records that "fifty-one gallons and a half of the best Malaga wine were consumed by the mourners." In 1685, at the funeral of the Rev. Thomas Cobbett, the minister in Ipswich, one barrel of wine and two barrels of cider were consumed, and "as it was cold," there was "some spice and ginger for the cider." The outright drunkenness of the beloved minister's parishioners is hard to imagine, but the excessive drinking was quite a common practice in the days before temperance and prohibition. In the case of a pauper's death, the towns would provide and bear the expense of intoxicating drinks. For example, in 1728 in Salem at the funeral of a pauper, a gallon of wine and another of cider are charged as "incidental," and in the following year, six gallons of rum for a funeral was provided by the town. In Lynn, it was documented in 1711 that the town furnished "half a barrel of cider for the Widow Dispaw's funeral." A careful, and above all, experienced committee was appointed to supervise the mixing of the funeral grog or punch, and to attend to the liberal and frequent dispensing of it to the mourners. It is an odd to imagine the spectral visions that people may have seen had they overindulged themselves in drinking, associating ghosts to the deceased, when perhaps it had come from their own drunken delusions. When David Porter of Hartford, Connecticut, drowned in 1678, the bill for the expenses of the recovery and burial of his body included liquor for those who dived for him, for those who brought him home, and included the jury of inquest. It was written in local records that eight gallons and three quarts of wine and a barrel of cider were consumed. The sheet and coffin used at this funeral cost thirty shillings, however, the liquor that was consumed came to more than twice that sum. Throughout New England, bills for funeral goods included large sums for items such as rum, cider, whiskey, lemons, sugar, and spices. Many families bore the cost of libations at a funeral for several years after the body was interred in the cold ground.

In Nathaniel Hawthorne's *Twice Told Tales*, he reflected on the behavior of New Englanders at funerals:

> They were the only class of scenes, so far as my investigation has taught me, in which our ancestors were wont to steep their tough old hearts in wine and strong drink and indulge in an outbreak of grisly jollity.
>
> Look back through all the social customs of New England in the first century of her existence and read all her traits of character, and find one occasion other than a funeral feast where jollity was sanctioned by universal practice.... Well, old friends! Pass on with your burden of mortality and lay it in the tomb with jolly hearts. People should be permitted to enjoy themselves in their own fashion; every man to his taste—but New England must have been a dismal abode for the man of pleasure when the only boon-companion was Death.

TELLING THE BEES

Upon the death of a family member, it was customary to go out and speak to the beehive and inform the bees. This custom was based on the superstition that the bees were "souls" and they could fly up to heaven whence they came looking for the deceased. This tradition was very common throughout New England and began in Colonial times. There was even the idea that if the bees were not told of the death, then someone else in the household would die. The straw beehives would be draped with mourning cloth or crepe to signify the death.

The bees in those times, much like cats and dogs, were a part of the family, and were supposed to possess occult knowledge, and so the bees played a part of the family's bereavements. When a loved one died, the survivor would go out into the garden and knock on the hives, giving the news to the inhabitants.

The poem by John Greenleaf Whittier, called "Telling the Bees," describes the custom:

Before them under the garden wall,
Forward and back,
Went drearily singing the chore-girl small,
Draping each hive with a shred of black.
Trembling, I listened: the summer sun
Had the chill of snow,
For I knew she was telling the bees of one
Gone on the journey we all must go.
And the song she was singing, ever since
In my ear sounds on
Stay at home, pretty bees, fly not hence!
Mistress Mary is dead and gone!

DEATH, POSSESSION, AND A GRAVEYARD

Susie Smith was the seventeen-year-old daughter of Doctor Greenleaf Smith of Lawrence, Massachusetts. The strange occurrence upon her death during the 1800s cannot be explained to this day. A popular girl with many friends, Susie was the organist at Webster Hall in Lawrence. Susie had taken ill one day, and on a gloomy Wednesday she awoke from a very deep sleep and exclaimed, "Father, I've attended my own funeral." The experience she described was all too real and vivid to Susie. She spoke of such details in the experience including the hymns that were sung by the mourners in attendance. Her family sat and listened to the grim details of her story in amazement.

That night at 6:00 p.m., Susie succumbed to her ailment, and her body shook in violent spasms. In a few moments she was gone and upon her face was a pale, lifeless expression. Susie's family stood silent over her body and wept at their loss. The heartbreaking scene was disturbed by a deep, gruff voice breaking the silence, "Rub both of her arms as hard as you can," the voice said. The Doctor rubbed Susie's arm repeatedly, obeying the mysterious command.

A second voice, different than the first, instructed the Doctor to "Raise her up." Susie's father reached around her lifeless body and propped her up and sat behind her. Amazingly the girl began to breathe. Yet, another voice spoke out, "If I could move her legs around so that I could set her up on the footboard, she'd be all right." Before the Doctor could move Susie's legs, an unseen force lifted her legs and placed them on the footboard.

Then Susie's body seemed possessed by a friendly and energetic spirit, which was different from the others. This spirit moved Susie back into her original position on her deathbed. Time crept slowly by as the family sat awestruck, wondering what was going to happen next. A fifth spirit came forth, and this one wanted to talk. The conversation from this spirit was alleged to have continued for three hours into the night. The voice informed the family that Susie's body had been possessed by spirits. Susie appeared to be in a deep sleep once again. In the morning the girl's eyes opened and another spirit spoke through her and asked the question, "Who am I?" Her panic-stricken father exclaimed, "You are Susie Smith." The spirit quickly replied and said, "No, I ain't. Susie Smith died last night." The story goes that for the remainder of the day, this spirit spoke through Susie, maintaining that Susie was indeed dead. When evening fell, Susie was entranced in another deep sleep. On Friday morning the body of Susie continued to have episodes, and her exhausted family tried to come to terms with what was happening. Finally, at noontime, the strange life that inhabited Susie's body was gone, and she was dead and cold once again.

The following morning, Dr. Smith had Susie's body prepared for burial, convinced that she really was gone this time. The family tried to decide where to bury Susie in discussions that took place in a lower room of the house. Astonishingly, during the discussion, an apparition of Susie stepped into the room, and as if she knew exactly what they had been talking about, she simply said, "Right on the School Hill; right on the side of the road." The spirit, who could clearly be heard walking into the room, vanished without a trace before the family's eyes. The family respected the guidance of the spirit in selecting the final resting place for Susie. Just outside of Fryeburg, Maine, in the town of Denmark, Susie was laid to rest on a recently selected cemetery lot, situated on a schoolhouse hillside.

DEATH WATCH

In the old colonial houses on Cape Cod, the sound of a wood tick beetle was believed to be an omen of death. Known as the death watch beetle, it has a hard case upon its head, with which it taps upon any hard substance, in many instances, coming through the floorboards of the old homes. In reality the ticking is the call to other insects in its species, in the same way that cricket noises are a note of communication with other crickets. There is a superstition linked with the death watch beetle, which, like many superstitions, is based upon the theory of probabilities. The death watch sound is usually heard in the springtime, and the belief is that someone in the house will die before the year ends. Those who were superstitious who heard the sound knew that it was a portent of things to come. The sounds of the beetle foretold of a coming death to the person who heard it. While the little beetle was just tapping to call his mate, and perhaps peeping into every corner and crevice of the house to find her, his actions caused fear and panic in the listener unlucky enough to hear him.

TRAPPINGS OF THE SPIRIT

When there was a corpse in the house, you had to cover or turn all the mirrors towards the wall so as not to trap the soul in the house. Another reason for doing this was to keep the living from seeing the dead in the mirror, which was a sure sign of another death in the family. If a mirror in your house was to fall and break by itself, it also meant that someone in the home would die soon. Domestic servants, and particularly superstitious persons, were quite often thrown into a panic by accidents of this sort. When someone died in the house and there was a clock in the room, the clock had to be stopped at the death hour or the family of the household would have bad luck. Windows and doors that were closed in the home would be opened up upon the death of someone in the house, so that their spirit would be free to leave.

AN IRONIC DEATH FOR THE STONE CARVERS OF BARRE, VERMONT

Barre, Vermont, welcomes visitors with a sign declaring that is the "Granite Capital of the World." Indeed a vast majority of granite monuments in the United States come from Barre. The Hope Cemetery is located on a small hillside in Barre, and is almost as famous as the town itself. The cemetery contains dozens of monuments memorializing Barre's own stone carvers. Walking through the Hope Cemetery, it is quickly evident that this is not your typical cemetery. Many people consider the cemetery an unusual gallery of artwork.

Consisting of sixty-five acres, Hope Cemetery was established in 1895. The original architectural plan for the cemetery was designed by Edward P. Adams, a nationally known landscape architect. The careful planning and high architectural standards of Hope reflect the most progressive principles in cemetery design and development. Today, there are over ten thousand monuments throughout the grounds made of Barre gray granite.

Barre was known around the world for its master granite craftsmen. Many of the stone carvers were of Italian descent. These master craftsmen were talented artists who worked the solid stone into pieces of grace and beauty. Unfortunately, most of the carvers died in their forties. While the marvels of granite were being created, the dust generated by that process was killing them. A lung disease called tuberculo-silicosis was the cause of death for countless stone carvers buried in the Hope Cemetery.

The detail in the monuments and markers is astonishing. In addition to crosses and cherubs, the monuments include a race car, pyramids, an airplane, an oversize soccer ball, and a six-foot-tall letter "A."

One of the most intriguing stones is for Elia Corti. Cut from a single piece of granite by the brother of the deceased, this hand-carved life-size figure with tremendous detail seems to come to life. The sculpture features small details from the creases in his trousers to the delicate moustache on his face. At Elia's feet is an assortment of life-size stone-carving tools. The grave for William and Gwendolyn Halvosa is a life-size granite bed. A man and woman are depicted sitting up in bed in pajamas, holding hands, their tomb stretched out before them.

Hope Cemetery is not only a resting place for the dead, but a showcase of stunning sculpture and art. And, ironically, it was the creation of that art that caused the death of many of the cemetery's inhabitants.

DEATH KEEPS THYME

In central Massachusetts, about twenty-five miles outside of Worcester, is the town of Lunenburg. Settled in 1719, it was called Turkey Hill (from a hill in the middle of the tract which was once frequented by wild turkeys) until the time of its incorporation, in 1728, when the name of Lunenburg was selected for the town by King George II from a German dominion he owned. Many of the first settlers were emigrants from Ireland and Scotland. A church was formed here in 1728, and soon after the south burial ground was established. The beautiful grounds offer ancient stones with elaborate carvings and fantastic epitaphs, such as the wonderful epitaph of Mr. and Mrs. Houghton:

Here lies the bodies of
Mr. Eleazer Houghton & Mrs. Elizabeth, his wife.
He died Feb. 20, 1790 in the Hundredth Year of his age &
She died June 27, 1785 in the 92 year of her age.
They was born in Lancaster & moved to Lunenburg in the year 1726.
They liv'd together a married life sixty nine years,
And upwards. He lived a peaceable
& pious life & never had a law-suit in all his life.

By this you see we are but dust
Prepare for death and follow us.

A large, old tree stands at the entrance to the graveyard and the low branches seem to reach out endlessly across the tops of the old tombstones. The burial ground is fascinating to walk around, not only for the visual effect, but also for the sensory effect. Immediately noticeable is a pungent smell of spice in the area. Looking across the hilly grounds you can see a thick carpet of creeping thyme as far as the eye can see.

The name "thyme" was first given to the plant by the Greeks as a derivative of a word which meant "to fumigate," either because they used it as incense, for its balsamic odor, or because it was taken as a type of sweet-smelling herb. Other origins of the name come from the Greek word "thumus," signifying courage. Among the Greeks, thyme denoted graceful elegance. "To smell of thyme" was an expression of praise, applied to those whose style was admirable. It was once thought that the souls of the dead dwell within the flowers of thyme. An old tradition says that thyme was one of the herbs that formed the fragrant bed of the Virgin Mary. In ancient Egypt, embalmers used thyme to ready mummies for their heavenly journeys. The ancient Greeks would burn thyme in their sacred rituals because of its aromatic smell, and Roman soldiers bathed in thyme water to renew energy. In Medieval days, thyme was also a symbol of bravery and courage, and ladies would embroider a bee hovering over sprigs of thyme onto a scarf and offer it to their knight. During the Middle Ages, people drank concoctions of thyme to treat them against leprosy, the plague, body lice, coughs, and digestive problems.

In ancient legends and lore, thyme was associated with both death and funerals, yet it was also thought to have the ability to attract fairies. Thyme would be placed in coffins and graves as part of the burial ceremony. The strong scent of thyme was also used to mask the decay of the corpse. In this old burial ground, thyme seems more than appropriate for the gathering of spirits gone by.

DRESSED FOR DEATH

In Colonial times one of the chief expenses of a funeral was gloves, and a pair of gloves was sent as an invitation to attend the ceremony. In some documented cases, as many as one thousand pairs were given away, and often a man would record in his will the quality and cost of the gloves to be provided for his funeral. Sometimes pallbearers were given better gloves than those who had attended the services. It was written that at one Massachusetts funeral, seven hundred pairs of gloves were sent for one ceremony, and at another, three thousand were sent. So many gloves were received by persons of wide social connections that considerable revenue was derived from the sales of them. During the eighteenth century, one man sold his collection of three thousand funeral gloves for $640. Scarves, oftentimes made of silk, were given to the pallbearers, ministers, and others, and were worn for a considerable time after the funeral as a badge of respect for the dead.

In the nineteenth century, mourning rituals allowed New Englanders to demonstrate proper respect for the dead and served several purposes for those still living. Black mourning clothes had to be made very quickly following a death. The purpose of the clothing, besides being worn to the funeral, was to express sorrow and communicate a family's loss to the community without having to reiterate the details of the death. The color black was also thought to keep the roaming spirits from being able to inhabit a live person, as they could not see the body when dressed in black. The mourning period generally lasted six months to a year, depending on the relationship of the deceased to the mourner. The return to regular clothing then signaled the end of the deepest period of grief and the mourner's return to a normal routine.

It was also thought if someone was to try on mourning clothes, when not needing to wear them for a funeral, they would have occasion to wear it soon. To put on a hat of someone that was in mourning was a sign that one would need to be worn before the year was out. A legend from Maine tells that if a woman who was sewing puts her thimble on a table as she sits down to eat, it was a sign that she will be left a widow if she married. It was also believed that the clothes of the dead never lasted and wore out very quickly when used by the living. One belief was if someone put clothes of a live person on a corpse, when the clothes decayed, the owner would die.

FOR WHOM THE BELL TOLLS

The tolling of a "death bell" in New England was an announcement immediately upon the death of a person during the seventeenth and eighteenth centuries. The ringing of bells was thought to drive away all the evil spirits that might overcome the deceased, which they believed were always hovering round the dying to make a prey of their souls. The sound of the tolling bell was supposed to strike evil beings with terror and usher them away. Some people at their dying moment, who could afford to pay a large sum, would have the largest bell that was available. The belief was that the greater the noise, the more effective the ringing of the bell.

It was recorded in Sullivan, New Hampshire, in 1860, that upon a death, the bell was tolled for a quarter of an hour or more, with long intervals between the strokes of nearly a minute in length. Once the tolling was finished, the bell would be struck for each year of the deceased person's age. After another pause, a single stroke was given if the person were a male and two strokes if a female. However, it was not customary to toll for infants who were under three years of age. On the day of the burial, if the procession passed by the church, the bell was tolled while they passed. After the bell was installed in 1860, it was first tolled for the death of Henry H. Keith, on the afternoon of December 6. While away from his home in Sullivan, he had died the previous day at Saxton's River, Vermont. The bell was tolled as his funeral procession passed the church, on December 7th. After 1881, the bell was only tolled by request. Then, after 1891, the town made no provision to continue the tolling, and it was rarely used in relation to death and funerals.

On November 16, 1829, in Waterbury, Connecticut, a tax of one and one-half cents on the dollar was passed for the purchase of a bell, payable the first day of the following March. The old bell was at length broken by undue ringing one Christmas Eve, and it was decided to hang a new one before the installation of a pastor, which was to soon take place. A bell was sent from New York, but when it was tested one week before it was due to be installed, it was deemed unsatisfactory. The town decided to ride over to Hartford that afternoon to procure another one, and return that evening. The weather that night was intensely cold and the snow was drifting very heavily, but the team of two men equipped themselves with shovels and blankets, and left for Hartford.

While crossing the Southington plains, the drifting snow was so deep that the men had to shovel the paths for long distances, and they finally reached Hartford at nightfall. The men purchased a bell with tones that they liked and turned around for the tedious homeward drive of thirty miles over the mountain, with the bell in the sleigh—an additional weight of more than half a ton. At midnight the men had finally made it over the crest of the mountain, but not without a lot of shoveling and urging of the horses. At that point the road was so blockaded with snow that they couldn't travel with the sleigh. They decided to ride home on horseback, leaving the bell behind, but the snow was flying so badly they kept falling off their horses and the freezing cold only worsened their attempts. The men found a house that would take them in for the next night, because of the Sabbath being on Saturday, they had to wait until Sunday to attempt moving the bell again. Finally with the help of oxen, the sleigh was movable and the bell was delivered to Waterbury where it was installed two days later.

Long afterward the bell called the people to worship and gave them notice of occurring deaths. The bell was rung in groups of two strokes to give notice of the funeral when held in the church, and sometimes when held at private houses, and it was very slowly tolled while the body was being carried to its last resting place.

If a church bell chimed when no one had touched it, the superstition was that someone in the parish would die before that week was out. For sailing ships, the bell was the embodiment of the vessel's soul. When a ship met its fate on the seas, stories were told about hearing the bell sounding long after the entire ship was consumed by the waves. Many people visiting the graves of sea captains recalled hearing an ominous sound of bell tolling coming from the ground when there should have been no noise, perhaps as a reminder of the Captain's close relationship with the sea.

DANCING ON THE GRAVE

One of the most commonly told graveyard legends in Maine concerned a little, old seaport town along the Penobscot River known as Bucksport. Interred in a small family plot near the center of town is the grave of Colonel Johnathan Buck, which is marked by a tall granite marker with a curious image on it. The inscription on the stone reads:

CoL. Johnathan Buck

The Founder of Bucksport A.D.

1762

Born in Haverhill, Mass

1718.

Died March 18, 1795

On the other side of the monument is the single word "BUCK."

The stone shows no carved images by the stonecutter. However, there is one ingrained image that appeared within months of the marker being erected back in 1795: it is clearly the outline of a foot, just above the Buck name. The stories behind this mysterious foot have brought the town a bit of notoriety, especially from those interested in old Maine legends.

The most commonly told story about the Buck grave describes the founding father of the town as an austere and strict man, who was the highest civil authority in the settlement. Uncompromising, Colonel Buck held to the strong Puritan belief system and he would not suffer a reported witch in his community. An old woman, an outsider in the community, was the focus of such an accusation. The people of the town accused the woman of witchcraft, and she soon faced trial for her misdeeds and for being in league with evil incarnate. Immediately, Colonel Buck ordered her to be imprisoned, and some even say tortured to confess her crimes. Despite the fact that the woman would not confess, she was served with a speedy trial where she was found guilty of witchcraft and sentenced to execution.

The gallows, according to local record, were on the rocky hill across from the cemetery in town. As she was escorted to the gallows, the story goes that she cursed the judge for ordering her death and pleaded for her life. Those at the scene said that Colonel Buck motioned to the officers to hasten her to the gallows. The hangman prepared the old woman for her execution, and in her last moments on earth it is said that she uttered a curse that still resounds through the town today:

> Jonathan Buck, listen to these words, the last my tongue shall utter. It is the spirit of the only true and living God which bids me speak them to you. You will soon die. Over your grave they will erect a stone, that all may know where the bones of the mighty Jonathan Buck are crumbling to dust. But listen! Listen all ye people—tell it to your children and your children's children—upon that stone will appear the imprint of my foot, and for all time long, long after your accursed race has perished from the earth, the people will come far and near and the unborn generations will say, 'There lies the man who murdered a woman.' Remember well, Jonathan Buck, remember well!

The hangman then carried out his duty with the curse still hanging in the air.

Years later some people think that curse has come to pass and is evidenced by viewing the Buck grave marker. The panel of the pedestal that is most easily viewed from afar depicts the faint outline of a foot that perhaps some supernatural draughtsman had sketched upon the granite. Over the years people have traveled many distances to come and see the grave, and view the witch's curse for themselves. It has been said that numerous attempts have been made to remove what some consider a "stain," but whenever efforts are made to clean the stone, the mark only appears more vivid. Some accounts state that the stone has actually been changed several times, and yet the foot reappears in the same place as before. The theory was that the witch was dancing on the grave of the unsympathetic Colonel, as she had stated in her curse. Many non-believers say that the marking on the stone is accidental, or perhaps a flaw in the granite, and that the whole story is legend. There are those who state legend was made to fit the foot, nothing more. However the image is unmistakable on the gravestone and it does conjure up the story of the old woman's curse.

THE INSPIRING AND YET HUMBLE GRAVE OF CHAMPERNOWNE

On Gerrish's Island at the mouth of the Piscataqua River in Kittery, Maine, there is a random pile of stones that mark, according to legend, the last resting place of Francis Champernowne, a former owner and resident of the island. Champernowne was also the friend and relative of Sir Walter Raleigh, and by some was considered "the noblest born and bred of all New Hampshire's first planters." The story goes on further to say that he forbade any monument raised to his memory. Despite the fact that he was a man of distinction, personal worth, and noble blood, as he was the nephew to Sir Ferdinando Gorges, one of the original founders of Maine, he wanted no gravestone or marker to stand on his grave, only a pile of stones from the rockbound, sea-drenched Maine coast.

John Elwyn, a local resident who visited the grave every single year until he could no longer walk, wrote this of Champlain's tale:

Thomas De Cambernon for Hastings' field
Left Normandy; his tower saw him no more!
And no crusader's warhorse, plumed and steeled,
Paws the grass now at Modbury's blazoned door;
No lettered marble or ancestral shield, -
Where all the Atlantic shakes the lonesome shore,

Lies ours forgotten: only cobblestones
To tell us where are Champernowne's poor bones.

Dr. William Hale of Dover, New Hampshire, penned a very plaintive mourning song:

Where, wind to wave, and wave to echoing rock,
Their endless dirges chant for the lost renown;
With every bursting wave sounding a knell,
Above the lonely grave of Champernowne.

A Penny on Your Grave for Happiness, Montpelier, Vermont

The Greenmount Cemetery, located in Montpelier, Vermont, is the final resting place for little Margaret Pitkin. Margaret's plot is easily found because of a life-size statue of her standing over her grave. In 1899, Little Margaret died at the age of six from spinal meningitis. Margaret's parents contracted a local sculptor to carve a statue in her image, and they gave him her photograph to use as a reference.

Upon visiting the grave of little Margaret, you will see dozens of pennies tucked into small spaces on her sculpture. The belief is that leaving a penny on Margaret's grave is a prayer for her eternal happiness. In 1985, songwriter Dan Lindner was so inspired by Margaret's statue he wrote, "Song for Margaret."

An excerpt is as follows:

Silent she stands in her old fashioned dress, just a small figure
frozen in time,
Patient and calm as the world struggles on, for she's left all her
cares far behind.
And many who wander by her grave on the hill stop and leave her
a penny or two,
And each copper coin bears a wish and a prayer for the happiness
that she once knew.

THE CURSE FROM BEYOND THE GRAVE

In Salem, Massachusetts, the tragedies of the witch trials of 1692 intertwine with modern day commercialism. Ghost tours shuffle visitors from place to place, and on every corner there are shops that offer fortune-telling services to the inquisitive. Salem is a city that has long been a destination for those fascinated with this dark chapter from New England's history.

Giles Corey was one of six men executed during the Salem witch hysteria. Giles was eighty years old, and was married to Martha, who also was tried and put to death for practicing witchcraft. Giles maintained his innocence and pleaded not guilty, but he refused to be tried in court, as he felt the jury was already predisposed to a "guilty" verdict. Many people speculated that Corey refused to stand trial because he was afraid his land would be taken, while others believed that he refused out of sheer rebellion.

Sheriff George Corwin and his deputies brought Giles out to a pit in a grassy field and forced him to lie down. This pit was in an area that became the Howard Street Cemetery in 1801. A door was placed over Giles and large rocks were piled up on top of it to press a "confession" out of him. Giles refused to confess by remaining mute despite the crushing weight of the rocks. Near the end of the second day, after repeated questioning, Giles just responded with "more weight." As the body of Giles Corey responded to the weight, his eyes bulged and his tongue popped out of his mouth. Sheriff Corwin pushed Giles' tongue back in with his cane. With his dying breath, Giles cursed the Sheriff and the town of Salem.

The curse has come true, according to Robert Cahill, a local historian and former sheriff of Essex County. Robert Cahill has spent a lot of time chronicling the history following Corey's curse. When Robert was interviewed by the History Channel, he pointed out that each and every sheriff, starting with George Corwin up to himself, had either died in office or was forced into early retirement due to a heart or blood ailment.

The Howard Street Cemetery is the place where the ghost of Giles Corey is most often seen. In 1914, Salem residents reported seeing the ghost of Giles at the cemetery just before the Great Fire of the same year. Coincidentally, the Great Fire of 1914 began on Gallows Hill where nineteen witches were hanged. Visitors to the cemetery often capture strange phenomenon in their photos, including ghostly shapes.

Looming ominously at the edge of the cemetery is the old Salem Jail, built in 1811. One of the oldest correctional facilities in the country, it was vacated in 1991 and stands abandoned, casting a dark shadow across the grounds. The cemetery is largely neglected with bushes overtaking the slate stones and trash scattered about. Those who visit Salem seeking historic cemeteries often visit old Burying Point on Charter Street, which dates from 1637, but not many people know that just few streets over is a haunted cemetery that harkens back to Salem's infamous legacy.

DON'T DISTURB THE DEAD

Located north of Boston in Essex County is the picturesque town of Newburyport, Massachusetts. After the settlement of the town in 1635, it soon became a fishing and trading community. The Old Hill Burying Ground was established in 1729 on a prominent high point in the town. The land is quite steep and is being undermined by numerous gopher holes. The burial ground is filled with notable people from Newburyport's history. There are hundreds of old slanting and falling tombstones throughout the grounds.

Alongside of the hill is the large Pierce tomb that houses members of that family who died of tuberculosis between 1863 and 1899. It is immediately evident that the door to the tomb has been resealed in recent years. This tomb has been opened by vandals at least three times since 1925. The first time, vandals gained entrance to the tomb by digging an opening behind the tomb and breaking their way through the crumbling stonework. According to records, the youths opened the coffins and removed the clothes from the corpses, put them on, and danced around the burial ground. The corpses were also propped up to a seated position and surrounded by lit candles as they were poked with sticks. The vandals were finally reported to the police after being spotted in the decayed clothing and they confessed to their deed. The clothing was placed back on the corpses and the tomb was closed up.

In 1985, vandals broke into the same tomb again, this time setting it up as a clubhouse. They brought in alcohol and poured it into the corpses mouths and took all of the rotting clothing off of them, as they observed the alcohol pouring out of the body. The caretaker to the grounds found that the tomb had been broken into and alerted the police. The police made a public appeal on the front page of the local newspaper for the vandals to come forward. The vandals confessed and were brought immediately to the hospital to be examined as the bodies they had disturbed had died from contagious diseases. The three boys did not contract any of the diseases according to records.

In 2005, a man doing court-ordered community work in the burial ground kicked in the entrance of the Pierce tomb. He twisted a skull of off one of the skeletons and posed for pictures with it. He showed the skull to the other community service workers who ran away upon seeing it. When he was done playing with the skull, he kicked it down the hill, where it was later recovered in an animal hole. Police could not identify the dismembered corpse because the silver nameplates that accompany each body in the crypt had been stolen in the previous break-in. The court sentenced the man to two and a half years in jail for the crime and the tomb was sealed once more.

Over the years people have claimed to see two ghostly figures walking right through the door of the Pierce tomb and crossing the burial ground. Some people believe that they have captured infrared photographs of the ghosts walking in to the door of the tomb. Many residents believe that the tomb is the center of ghostly activity in the burial ground because of all the vandalism over the years. Perhaps it's best not to disturb the graves of the dead, as they may end up haunting the living.

THE GHOST BRIDE OF CAPE ELIZABETH

The sad and haunting tale of Lydia Carver can be found in a tiny graveyard located next to the Inn by the Sea in Cape Elizabeth, Maine. The tallest gravestone there tells the unfortunate story:

> Sacred to the memory of Miss Lydia Carver,
> daughter of Mr. Amos Carver of Freeport.
> At 21, who with 15 other unfortunate passengers,
> male and female, perished in the merciless waves
> by the shipwreck of the Schooner Charles.
> Capt. Isaac Adams bound from Boston to Portland
> on a reef of rocks near the shore of Richmond Island
> on Sunday night, July 12, 1807.

The circumstances surrounding Lydia's death are especially tragic. Lydia had sailed with her bridal party on the schooner *Charles* on an overnight trip from Portland, Maine, to Boston. Lydia was excited about the trip, as she was going to be fitted for her bridal gown. During the return trip, the weather abruptly turned from sunny to stormy. A severe gale blew in and tossed the *Charles* on to an area of rocks known at Watt's Ledge just fifty feet offshore from Richmond Island. The waves overcame the ship and knocked it on its side. The terrified passengers tried to cling to the masts and rigging as wind and furious waves washed over the wrecked schooner. Captain Adams and three other men desperately tried to reach Richmond's Island on their own. Adams's wife frantically called him back to the ship, but he was overtaken by the waves and sent to a watery grave. As the night wore on, the *Charles* began to break apart, washing those clinging for dear life into the relentless sea. The morning sunlight revealed a heart-wrenching scene: The body of Lydia Carver washed ashore on Crescent Beach. Next to her was the trunk containing her never-to-be-worn wedding gown. Sixteen people in all perished that night in the waters off of Cape Elizabeth. The bodies of the captain and his wife were buried in the

Eastern Cemetery in Portland. Lydia is buried in the graveyard on at the top of the hill that overlooks Crescent Beach.

The gravestone for Lydia is over two hundred years old, yet it is in perfect condition. The people from the nearby Inn believe that Lydia takes care of her grave, keeping it clean and maintained. It is interesting to note that there are several other stones in the graveyard that date after 1807, and they are hardly discernable. Guests of the Inn have reported seeing a woman appear and disappear right before their eyes at Lydia's gravestone. A longtime member of the Cape Elizabeth Historical society reported that in the 1960s, her daughter saw Lydia standing alongside two deer on nearby Route 77, before the current Inn was built.

As the Inn by the Sea overlooks the Atlantic Ocean, it has become a popular place for weddings. Over the years, brides to be have reported being awoken during the night by Lydia. Some brides described seeing Lydia at the foot of their bed, while others have seen their wedding gowns move or float above them. However, in every encounter with Lydia's ghost, no one has reported being frightened. The folks at the Inn feel like Lydia is a permanent visitor and they often see her in mirrors or on the elevator.

Lydia has often been seen on Crescent Beach as well. In the 1980s, Mark Hardee and his wife were guests at the Inn by the Sea. Mark decided to take a sunset stroll, strangely enough on the evening of July 12. Mark described hearing a loud crack, like the splintering of a ship off in the distance. He then described hearing a woman's loud, piercing scream. As Mark looked around for the source of the sound, he heard more screams, and then off in the distance he saw a ship wrecked just beyond Richmond Island shrouded by wisps of fog. Mark called to his wife, who quickly ran to his side, but the apparition of the ship disappeared and the air became quiet. Later that evening, when Mark and his wife went back to the inn, they told the staff what had happened on the beach. Imagine their surprise when Lydia's story was told to them, and the staff's amazement when it was revealed that his wife's name was Lydia Carver Hardee.

Although guests stay at the Inn a short time, Lydia's spirit is always around. Brush past the bushes of beach roses bordering the graveyard, and stand silently at her stone and she may make herself known to you. If you don't find Lydia by her gravestone, take a walk along the beach at sunset, for you might find the ghost bride roaming along the peaceful shore.

PREMONITIONS OF DEATH

A tale of superstition, premonition, and murder took place in Wethersfield, Connecticut, in 1782. One of Wethersfield's most prominent merchants and respected citizens, William Beadle, moved from London, England, to America in 1762. He soon married and opened up a popular country store. As payments for goods, Mr. Beadle accepted Continental currency, which was America's first paper money and was printed by the Continental Congress to help a newly independent nation grow after the American Revolution. Mr. Beadle kept all of his savings at home, and in a few years, due to inflation and devaluation of the money, all that he had saved was worthless. Mr. Beadle continued to entertain guests, despite the fact that his family was in severe financial straits. A journal that he kept described his thoughts:

> If a man who has once lived well meant well and done well falls by accident into poverty and then submits to be laughed at and trampled on by a set of mean wretches as far below him as moon is below the sun I say if such a man submits he must become meaner than meanness itself and I sincerely wish he might have ten years to his natural life to punish him for his folly.

Rather than face what Mr. Beadle thought was the shame of poverty, he decided to commit suicide. He also thought that it would have been cruel to leave his wife and children to bear poverty alone after his death, so he decided to kill them too. On the night of December 10, 1782, he sent the housemaid on an errand to the doctor. He then killed his wife, son, and three daughters. The next morning the people of the town were shocked to learn the news.

At the time of their deaths, Mr. Beadle was fifty-two and his wife was thirty-two.

The people of Wethersfield were so disturbed that they demanded that Mr. Beadle's body be buried at a crossroads, with a stake driven through his heart. However, no one could decide where to bury Mr. Beadle's body, as no one wanted it near their house or property. Finally the body was buried between high and low water on the riverbank, with the bloody knife fastened to his chest. However, the body was washed out by the river and exposed. The body was then buried in a secret location, but was mysteriously discovered by playing children. Finally Mr. Beadle's body was buried in another secret location.

Friends that knew Mrs. Beadle recalled how she mentioned the horrible dreams she had been having that led up to the murder. In these dreams she saw her children lying dead from violence. According to some, these dreams may have had the effect of convincing Mr. Beadle that his contemplated act was appropriate. He also believed that his wife's dreams were inspired by Heaven to convince him that their deaths were justified, and that it was evidence of complete heroism to die by one's own act. He wrote in his journal, "The Deity would punish no one who was impatient to visit God and learn his will from his own mouth, face to face."

Another superstition was revealed in a letter from this time written by a gentleman in Wethersfield to a friend that indicated the darkness of Mr. Beadle's deed. He wrote that there was a beautiful, clear full moon the night before the murder. There was no moon and no sun visible in the sky from the time the murder took place until the moment when Mr. Beadle was buried. When Mr. Beadle was placed in the ground by the river, the letter described a sudden wind that blew in from the northwest, immediately dispelling the clouds and revealing a brilliant blue sky.

VAMPIRE GRAVES IN VERMONT

The green mountain state has two curious stories that relate to vampire superstition, which caused graves to be opened and gruesome acts to be committed to the bodies of the deceased. The first incident took place in a town called Manchester, located in southern Vermont, in 1793, and involved a beautiful young woman named Rachel Harris, who married Captain Isaac Burton. Although Rachel was in good health, it was less than a year after her wedding day when she became deathly ill and succumbed to consumption. Captain Burton remarried about a year after her death to Hulda Powel, who was also in good health at the time of her marriage, although some say she was not as beautiful as Rachel. Within months of the marriage, Hulda became ill as well, displaying the same symptoms as Rachel: coughing up blood, an ashen face, and extended lethargy. The notion came to some of the family and friends that perhaps a vampire had killed Rachel and was now going after Hulda.

Judge John S. Pettibone, who was a Probate Judge and represented Vermont in the General Assembly from 1822 to 1842, wrote the following in a manuscript that is in the possession of the Manchester Historical Society:

> They were induced to believe that if the vitals of the first wife could be consumed by being burned in a charcoal fire it would effect a cure of the sick second wife. Such was the strange delusion that they disinterred the first wife who had been buried about three years. They took out the liver, heart, and lungs, what remained of them, and burned them to ashes on the blacksmith's forge of Jacob Mead. Timothy Mead officiated at the altar in the sacrifice to the Demon Vampire who it was believed was still sucking the blood of the then living wife of Captain Burton. It was the month of February and good sleighing. Such was the excitement that from five hundred to one thousand people were present. This account was furnished me by an eye witness of the transaction.

Despite the actions taken on the body of Rachel, Hulda died on September 6, 1793.

Isaac Burton's grave can be found today in the scenic Dellwood Cemetery in Manchester. He is buried with his fourth wife, Dency Raymond. The unmarked grave of Rachel is believed to be somewhere on the village green where the courthouse can be found today.

The other well-known story of vampirism happened in the town of Woodstock, located in central Vermont, in the 1830s. The account of events has appeared in several publications, including *The Journal of American Folklore* and later in the *Boston Transcript*. A man by the name of Corwin had died from consumption. His body was buried in the Cushing cemetery. It wasn't long after Corwin's death that his brother became very ill, and it was determined that he had also been stricken with consumption. Some people believed that perhaps the dead brother was rising from the grave and coming back for fresh blood.

To be certain, the town disinterred the body of the dead Corwin brother and examined his heart. According to the town's leading Physician, Doctor Joseph Gallup, the heart contained its victim's blood, although there still is a bit of speculation as to how he came to that determination. According to the Vermont newspaper, *The Standard*, the heart was taken to the middle of Woodstock Green, where they kindled a fire under an iron pot, placed the heart inside, and burned it until it was nothing but ashes. Some of the ashes were mixed with bull's blood and fed to the dying Corwin, hoping that the curse would be broken and the blood elixir would save him. The ashes that were left in the pot were then buried under a seven-ton granite slab. Ten years later, people who were digging at the site encountered a sulfurous smell and smoke spewing forth from the ground. Strangely, there is no information as to whether the remaining Corwin brother lived after drinking the ghastly mix.

There are no gravestones in the Cushing cemetery that bear the Corwin name. Could it be that time and weather have worn away reminders of the past, hiding the dark deeds that happened back during the early nineteenth century? The seven-ton granite slab from the town green is also missing. Town records do indicate these people truly did exist, though all evidence points to the contrary. Perhaps there has been enough digging into the past and this mystery is best left alone.

Conclusion: Memory

The floor we tread is holy ground,
Those gentle spirits hovering round,
While our fair circle joins again
Its broken chain.

—Oliver Wendell Holmes, "Memorial Verses"

The winding roads of New England lead travelers through quaint country towns and bustling cities. Most people travel from place to place with a destination in mind, often passing by reminders of the past without a second glance. With so much history surrounding those who live in New England, it's so easy to take for granted cemeteries that are hundreds of years old. Burial grounds of the earliest settlers can be found everywhere from family plots under a singular tree in a farm field, to crowded seventeenth-century burial grounds in state capitals. Gravestones are succumbing to the slow decay of time, crumbling a little more with each passing year. The carvings and epitaphs slowly fade as years of exposure to the weather wash away the stone surfaces. Some burial grounds that were once beautiful with inviting walking paths are now overgrown and severely neglected, making them spooky places to visit. Some cemeteries have also become targets for vandals who easily damage defenseless tombstones.

As New England's cemeteries slowly disappear, so does a part of history. Records of early burial grounds are difficult to find as it is, so to lose gravestones or cemeteries entirely is a tremendous loss. There are a variety of preservation groups working to restore and preserve cemeteries. These groups are typically non-profit and have quite a challenge raising funds to renovate neglected or forgotten cemeteries. For example, the Friends of the Valley Cemetery in Manchester, New Hampshire, are desperately trying to restore a historic and once-pristine cemetery. Established in the mid 1800s, this Victorian-era cemetery once had a reputation as a beautiful picnic and walking area. Recreational visitors no longer visit the cemetery as they once did. A sparkling natural brook that once meandered through the grounds is now mixed with city sewage and is directed through an underground culvert to the Merrimack River. Family mausoleums and tombs are vandalized and spray-painted with graffiti that is difficult and costly to remove. The once-majestic and towering trees are falling down, posing a risk to the monuments and statues. The few people that do visit Valley Cemetery often claim to hear disembodied voices and the sounds of a woman crying emanating from the gothic chapel. Perhaps in some strange, unearthly way, these spirits are reminding visitors that they don't want to be forgotten.

Some graveyards are being rediscovered throughout New England. On Court Street, in busy downtown Portsmouth, New Hampshire, an African burial ground has been unearthed several times. There are believed to be approximately two hundred people of African descent that were buried there in the eighteenth century. In 2003, when the site was discovered while the city was doing sewer work, archaeologists removed seven coffins containing eight bodies. The determination was made that this burial ground for slaves was forgotten in the nineteenth century as homes and a road were built over it. However, there is only a small plaque memorializing the burial ground—there are no gravestones or markers. Strangely enough, there are several houses on Court Street that are reported to be haunted by ghosts.

If you look carefully in some cemeteries you can find piles of old, broken tombstones tucked at the base of stonewalls or under bushes. These gravestones in most cases will never be placed back over the graves where they belong as a reminder of who is buried there. Fallen gravestones sink further and further into the ground in some cemeteries soon to be consumed by the earth that surrounds them. In some cases, the memory and identity of those who died disappears along with their gravestones.

The preservation of New England's cemeteries is something that is slowly evolving, yet there are many that are still at risk, where there are no groups to save them. Efforts are being made to document many of the isolated burial grounds, but this is mostly done by volunteers, and with the sheer number of them hidden in woods or overgrown, many of them may never be found. Cemetery records that do exist often tell of more stones that are no longer standing or visible in many locations.

Someone once told me that you can't really tell where you're going unless you've first understood where you've been. Cemeteries show us where we've been, and who has passed down the roads before us. Perhaps the ghosts in these cemeteries are there not only to remind us of their own personal stories, but of our own past which seems to slip further away as the stones fade over the years.

Could it be that the ghosts in the cemeteries want to be sure that we remember them as their stones fade over the years and their stories are forgotten?

BIBLIOGRAPHY

Aimwell, Walter. *Our Little Ones in Heaven*, Gould and Lincoln Publishing, 1875.

Arrington, Benjamin. *Municipal History of Essex County in Massachusetts*. Lewis Historical Publishing, 1922.

Austin, Jane Goodwin. *Dr. LeBaron and His Daughters: A Story of the Old*. Houghton-Mifflin Publishing, 1892.

Bates, Arlo. *In the Bundle of Time*. Roberts Brothers Publishing, 1893.

Botkin, Benjamin Albert. *A Treasury of New England Folklore: Stories, Ballads, and Traditions of the Yankee People*. Crown Publishers, 1947.

Bridgman, Thomas. *Epitaphs from Copp's Hill Burial Ground, Boston: With Notes*. J. Munroe and Company Publishing, 1851.

Browne, Frances Fisher. *Golden Poems by British and American Authors*. A. C. McClurg & co. Publishers, 1914.

Burbank, Alfred Stevens. *Guide to Historic Plymouth: Localities and Objects of Interest*. A.S. Burbank Publishing, 1902.

Cahill, Robert. *Haunted Happenings: With New Photos of Old Ghosts*. Old Saltbox Publishing, 1992.

Chase, George Wingate. *The History of Haverhill, Massachusetts: From Its First Settlement, in 1640, to the Year 1860*. Published by the author, 1861.

Citro, Joseph A., and Diane Foulds. *Curious New England: The Unconventional Traveler's Guide to Eccentric Destinations*. UPNE Publishers, 2004.

Coe, Richard. *The Old Farm Gate: Containing Stories and Poems for Children and Youth*. Daniels and Smith Publishing, 1852.

Coffin, Robert Stevenson, *The Miscellaneous Poems of the Boston Bard*, J.H. Cunningham Publisher, 1818.

Crofut, Florence S. Marcy. *Guide to the History and the Historic Sites of Connecticut*. Yale University Press, 1937.

Cutter, Daniel Bateman. *History of the Town of Jaffrey, New Hampshire, from the Date of the Masonian Charter to the Present Time, 1749–1880*. Republican Press Association, 1881.

De Fontaine, Felix. T*he Fireside Dickens: A Cyclopedia of the Best Thoughts of Charles,* Dickens. Kessinger Publishing, 2004.

Drake, Samuel Adams. *New England Legends and Folklore in Prose and Poetry*. Little Brown and Company Publishers, 1910.

Earle, Alice Morse. *Customs and Fashions in Old New England*. Charles Scibner's Publishing, 1893.

Gately, Paul, "Who Haunts The Sagamore Cemetery," *Bourne Courier,* January 25, 2007.

Goold, William. *Portland in the Past: With Historical Notes of Old Falmouth*. Heritage Books, Inc., 1997.

Gordon, Dan and Gary Joseph. *Cape Encounters: Contemporary Cape Cod Ghost Stories*. Cockle Cove Press, 2004.

Griffith, George Bancroft. *The poets of Maine: A collection of specimen poems from over four hundred verse-makers of the Pine-tree state.* Pickard & Company Publishing, 1888.

Harbaugh, Henry. *Poems*. Lindsay & Blakiston Publishing, 1860.

Hawthorne, Hildegarde. *Old Seaport Towns of New England*. Dodd Publishing, 1916.

Hawthorne, Nathaniel, *The Complete Works of Nathaniel Hawthorne*, Houghton, Mifflin, New York, 1882.

Hodgon, George Enos, Thomas W. Hancock, and Richard Cutts Shannon. *Reminiscences and Genealogical Record of the Vaughan Family of New Hampshire*. Genesee Press, 1918.

Holland, Josiah Gilbert. *History of Western Massachusetts: The Counties of Hampden, Hampshire, Franklin, and Berkshire*. S. Bowles and company Publishing, 1855.

Irving, Washington. *The Works of Washington Irving.* G.P. Putnam's Sons Publishing, 1880.

Jones, Herbert G. *Old Portland Town.* The Machigonne Press, 1938. Knoblock, Glenn A. Portsmouth Cemeteries (Images of America). Arcadia Publishing, 2005.

Longfellow, Henry Wadsworth. *Poems of America.* Houghton-Mifflin and company, Publishing, 1878.

Ludwig, Allen. *Graven Images: New England Stonecarving and its Symbols, 1650–1815.* Wesleyan Press, 1966.

Mac Donald, Edward. *Old Copp's Hill and Burial Ground: With Historical Sketches.* Industrial School Press Publishing, 1891.

MacPherson, Rick. "Tales From the Boneyard." *Casco Bay Weekly,* October 26, 1995.

Mann, Henry. *The Land We Live in: Or, The Story of Our Country.* Christian Herald Publishing, 1896.

Marble, A.P. *The New England Magazine and Bay State Monthly.* J. N. McClintock, 1887.

Perkins, Frank Herman and Alfred Stevens Burbank. *Handbook of Old Burial Hill, Plymouth, Massachusetts: Its History, Its Famous Dead, and Its Quaint Epitaphs.* A.S. Burbank Publishing, 1902.

Rittenhouse, Jessie Belle. *The Little Book of American Poets, 1787–1900.* Houghton-Mifflin company, 1917.

Robinson, Edwin Arlington. *Collected Poems.* Macmillan Publishing, 1921.

Rogak, Lisa. *Stones and Bones of New England: A Guide to Unusual, Historic, and Otherwise Notable Cemeteries.* Globe Pequot Publishing, 2004.

Sheldon, George. *A History of Deerfield, Massachusetts: The Times when the People by Whom it was Settled, Unsettled and Resettled.* Press of E.A. Hall & co. Publishing, 1895.

Shepard, Odell. *The Harvest of a Quiet Eye.* Houghton-Mifflin Company, 1927.

Skinner, Charles *Montgomery. Myths and Legends of Our Own Land.* J.P. Lippincott Company Publishers, 1896.

Sprague, Charles. *Writings of Charles Sprague: Now First Collected.* C.S. Francis Publishing, 1843.

Stedman, Edmund Clarence, *The Poems of Edmund Clarence Stedman,* Houghton Mifflin Company, 1908.

Stephens, Harriet Marion. *Home Scenes and Home Sounds: Or, The World from My Window.* Fetridge and Company Publishing, 1854.

Thompson, Nathan David. *The Royal Gallery of Poetry and Art.* N.D. Thompson Publishing Co., 1886.

Warner, Francis Lester. *Pilgrim Trails: A Plymouth-to-Provincetown Sketchbook.* Atlantic Monthly Press, 1921.

Warren, Ed, Robert David Chase. *Graveyard: More Terrifying Than Stephen King—Because It's True!* Macmillan Publishing, 1993.

Wellesley College, Department of English Literature, Collected by Helen J Sanborn, *Persephone and Other Poems*, Fort Hill Press, 1905.

Whitman, Ruth. *Laughing Gas: Poems, New and Selected, 1963–1990.* Wayne State University Press, 1991.

Whittier, John Greenleaf. *The Poetical Works of John Greenleaf Whittier.* Houghton-Mifflin and company Publishing, 1891.

Worcester Mass Historical Society. *Proceedings of the Worcester Society of Antiquity.* Published by The Society, 1894.

RESOURCES

The Ancient Burying Ground Association,
www.theancientburyingground.org

Association for Gravestone Studies, www.gravestonestudies.org

A Very Grave Matter—Historic New England Burial Grounds,
www.gravematter.com

Banjo Dan and the Mid Nite Plowboys, www.banjodan.com

Connecticut Gravestone Network, www.ctgravestones.com

Gravestone Preservation Network, www.gravestonepreservation.info

Gray Maine's Stranger, 20thmainevolunteers.com/stranger.html
The Lost Village of Bara-Hack, bara-hack.com/

Maine Old Cemetery Association,
www.rootsweb.ancestry.com/~memoca/moca.htm

New England Curiosities, www.newenglandcuriosities.com
New Hampshire Old Graveyard Association,
www.rootsweb.ancestry.com/~nhoga

Rhode Island Historical Cemetery Commission,
www.historicalcemeteries.ri.gov

Spirits Alive, Friends of the Eastern Cemetery, Portland, Maine,
www.spiritsalive.org

The Vermonter, www.vermonter.com

Vermont Old Cemetery Association, www.sover.net/~hwdbry/voca/

About the Author

Roxie Zwicker is known for her unique collection of New England folklore and stories. She was born in Massachusetts and grew up in New England surrounded by it beauty and history. After attending Greenfield Community College for Media Production, Roxie found herself  exploring the hidden secrets of New England. Since 1993, she has captured audiences with her fascinating storytelling abilities. In 2002, she started her own business, New England Curiosities, giving tours in New Hampshire and Maine featuring many of the stories from her repetoire. Within just two years, Roxie and New England Curiosities were featured on the History Channel and the Travel Channel. She has also been in countless regional and national magazines, including *Better Homes and Gardens*. In 2007, her first book, *Haunted Portsmouth*, was released, which went into a second printing within months of its release, followed by *The Haunted Pubs of New England* and *Haunted Portland*. In 2009, Roxie will publish her most ambitious book to date, *Haunted Cemeteries of New England: Stories, Stones, and Superstitions*, which is a compilation of seven years of research and original photographs. Roxie's deep appreciation for authenticity and appreciation of history is evident in her writing. Roxie's website can be visited at www.newenglandcuriosities.com.